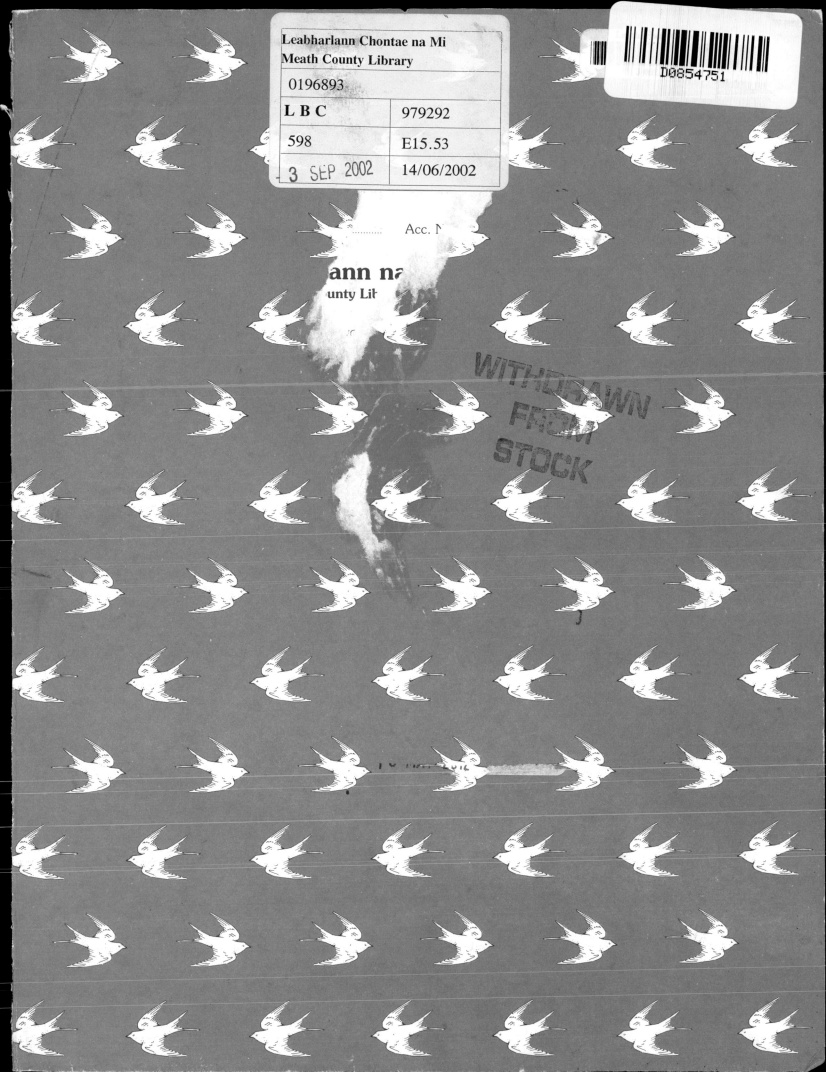

EYEWITNESS GUIDES

BIRD

Pheasant wing

Crow egg

Guillemot egg

Magpie egg

Wagtail nest

Mallard wing

Peacock tail covert

Budgerigar feathers

Dunnock egg Great tit egg

EYEWITNESS 👁 GUIDES

BIRD

Written by
DAVID BURNIE

Tawny owl skull

Mandarin duck display feather

Quail egg

Swallow egg

Blackbird skull

Golden pheasant cape feathers

Kittiwake egg

Macaw flight feather

Avocet skull

Starling egg

Jay wing feather

Bird of paradise display feathers

DK

DORLING KINDERSLEY • LONDON
in association with
THE NATURAL HISTORY MUSEUM • LONDON

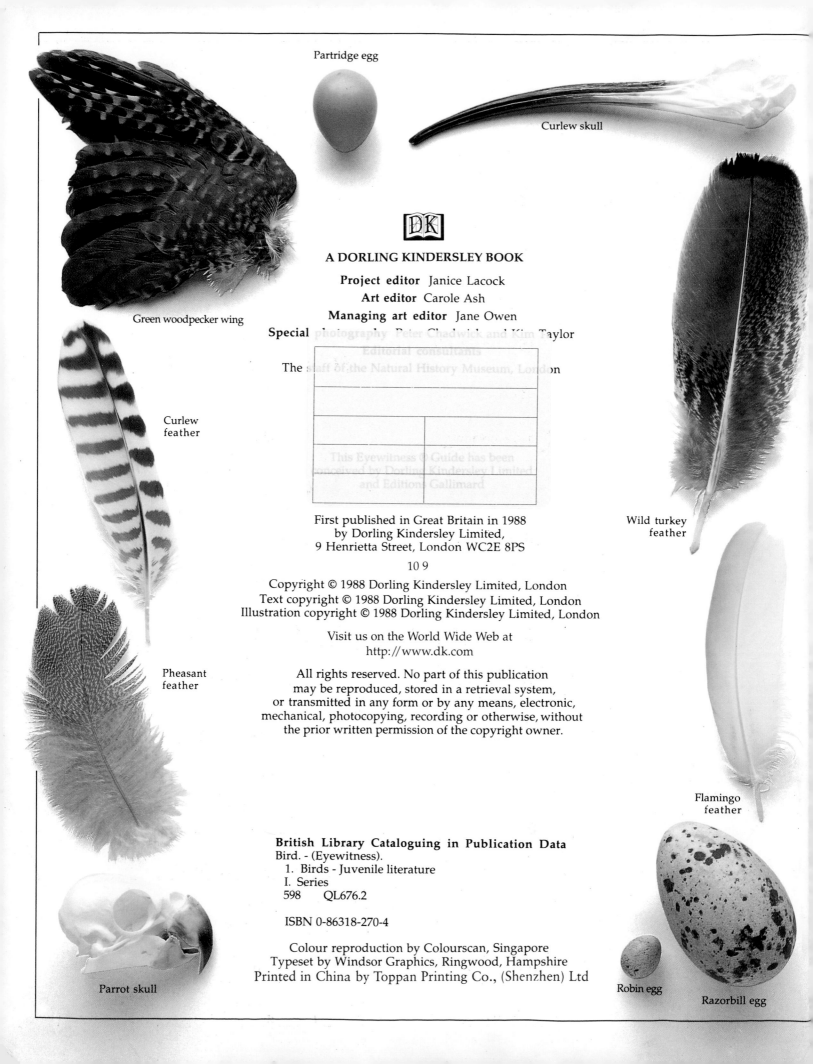

Partridge egg

Curlew skull

Green woodpecker wing

Curlew feather

Pheasant feather

Wild turkey feather

Flamingo feather

Parrot skull

Robin egg

Razorbill egg

DK

A DORLING KINDERSLEY BOOK

Project editor Janice Lacock
Art editor Carole Ash
Managing art editor Jane Owen
Special photography Peter Chadwick and Kim Taylor
Editorial consultants
The staff of the Natural History Museum, London

This Eyewitness ® Guide has been
conceived by Dorling Kindersley Limited
and Editions Gallimard

First published in Great Britain in 1988
by Dorling Kindersley Limited,
9 Henrietta Street, London WC2E 8PS

10 9

Visit us on the World Wide Web at
http://www.dk.com

British Library Cataloguing in Publication Data
Bird. - (Eyewitness).
1. Birds - Juvenile literature
I. Series
598   QL676.2

ISBN 0-86318-270-4

Colour reproduction by Colourscan, Singapore
Typeset by Windsor Graphics, Ringwood, Hampshire
Printed in China by Toppan Printing Co., (Shenzhen) Ltd

Contents

Rock pebbler feather

Cockatiel feather

Budgerigar feather

Archaeopteryx - the primaeval bird

From dinosaur to bird

TWO HUNDRED MILLION YEARS AGO, at a time when insects were the only flying animals, a small lizard-like creature gave up scuttling between the trees in which it lived, and instead took to gliding. It did this on small flaps of skin that acted like parachutes, and from this humble beginning, giant winged reptiles called pterosaurs gradually evolved. But membranous wings had their disadvantages: they were difficult to fold up when on the ground, and if they became torn, the chances of the creature being able to fly again were very small. Evolution's answer to this problem was the feather. In 1861, one of the world's most famous fossil animals, *Archaeopteryx*, was discovered. Although this creature lived over 150 million years ago, when the pterosaurs were still in their heyday, the fossils show that this crow-sized animal was thickly feathered. Unfortunately, nothing is known about the immediate descendants of *Archaeopteryx*. What is certain is that when the pterosaurs were mysteriously swept away with the dinosaurs, there followed a huge increase in bird species. Today, over 8,500 species of birds populate the skies.

THE MISSING LINK

The five *Archaeopteryx* fossils found in Germany in 1861 all came from an area which was once flooded by a sea. When the animals died, their bodies were rapidly covered by silt which was so fine that it preserved not only the outlines of bones, but also those of feathers. Over millions of years, this compressed silt gradually became limestone, and when it was quarried, the stone yielded up its precious fossils. In this fossil, the bird-like wings and legs are clearly visible, as are the reptilian teeth and tail. It is thought likely that *Archaeopteryx* evolved from small dinosaurs that ran upright instead of walking on all fours.

Wings

Tail

Legs

Teeth

EVOLUTIONARY EXPERIMENT

Although fossils show that pterosaurs were highly successful in their time, they all died out 65 million years ago. They were not directly related to the ancestors of modern birds.

STAYING BALANCED

Compared to many animals, birds are compact creatures. A bird's legs, wings and neck are all lightweight structures. The heavy parts, particularly its wing and leg muscles, are packed closely around the rib-cage and backbone. This allows a bird to stay balanced both on the wing and on the ground.

Front view of a crow's skeleton

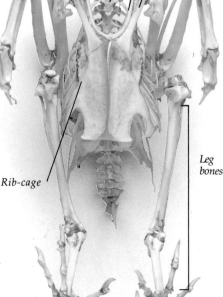

Skull

Neck

Backbone

Wishbone

Coracoid bone

Rib-cage

Leg bones

AS DEAD AS THE DODO

The dodo, here depicted in the famous fictional encounter with Lewis Carroll's heroine, Alice, in *Through the Looking Glass*, was one of many birds whose demise was caused by man. The dodo was a flightless bird of Madagascar and neighbouring islands in the Indian Ocean, and was driven to extinction in the late 17th century. Flying birds have also suffered at man's hands. The last passenger pigeon died in 1914, whereas 100 years earlier, the species formed flocks over a *billion* strong.

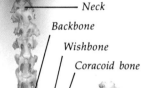

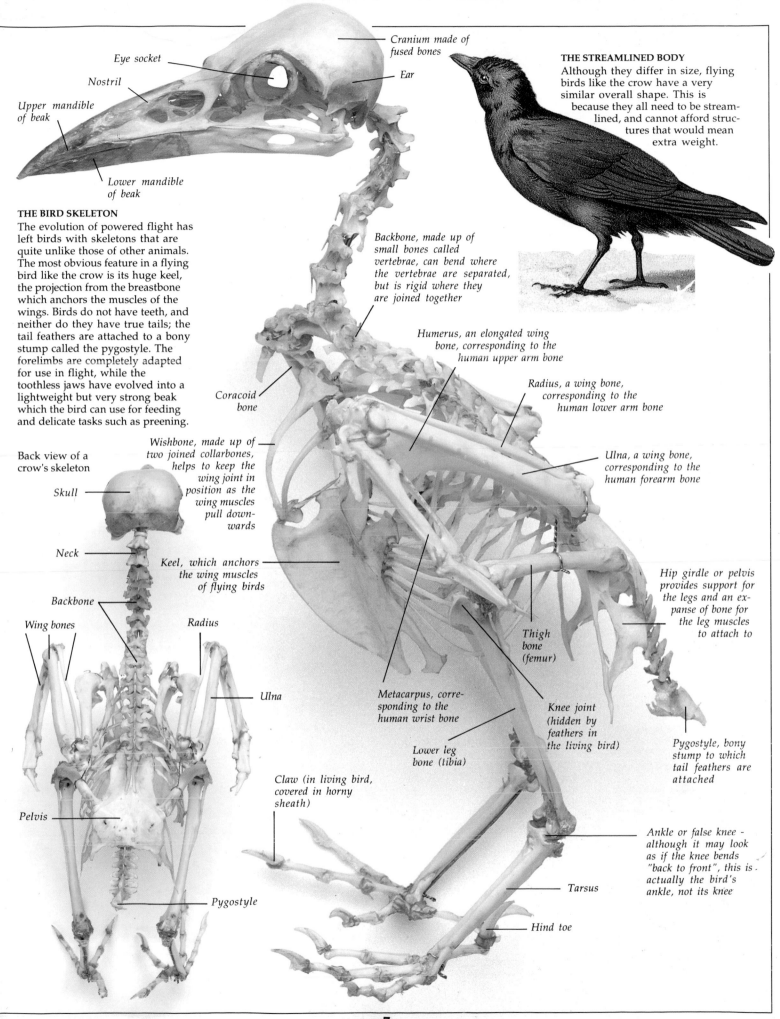

Eye socket

Nostril

Upper mandible
of beak

Cranium made of
fused bones

Ear

Lower mandible
of beak

THE STREAMLINED BODY
Although they differ in size, flying birds like the crow have a very similar overall shape. This is because they all need to be streamlined, and cannot afford structures that would mean extra weight.

THE BIRD SKELETON
The evolution of powered flight has left birds with skeletons that are quite unlike those of other animals. The most obvious feature in a flying bird like the crow is its huge keel, the projection from the breastbone which anchors the muscles of the wings. Birds do not have teeth, and neither do they have true tails; the tail feathers are attached to a bony stump called the pygostyle. The forelimbs are completely adapted for use in flight, while the toothless jaws have evolved into a lightweight but very strong beak which the bird can use for feeding and delicate tasks such as preening.

Back view of a
crow's skeleton

Skull

Neck

Backbone

Wing bones

Radius

Ulna

Pelvis

Pygostyle

Coracoid
bone

Wishbone, made up of
two joined collarbones,
helps to keep the
wing joint in
position as the
wing muscles
pull down-
wards

Keel, which anchors
the wing muscles
of flying birds

Backbone, made up of small bones called vertebrae, can bend where the vertebrae are separated, but is rigid where they are joined together

Humerus, an elongated wing bone, corresponding to the human upper arm bone

Radius, a wing bone, corresponding to the human lower arm bone

Ulna, a wing bone, corresponding to the human forearm bone

Hip girdle or pelvis provides support for the legs and an expanse of bone for the leg muscles to attach to

Thigh
bone
(femur)

Metacarpus, corresponding to the human wrist bone

Knee joint
(hidden by
feathers in
the living bird)

Lower leg
bone (tibia)

Claw (in living bird,
covered in horny
sheath)

Pygostyle, bony stump to which tail feathers are attached

Ankle or false knee - although it may look as if the knee bends "back to front", this is actually the bird's ankle, not its knee

Tarsus

Hind toe

Birds as animals

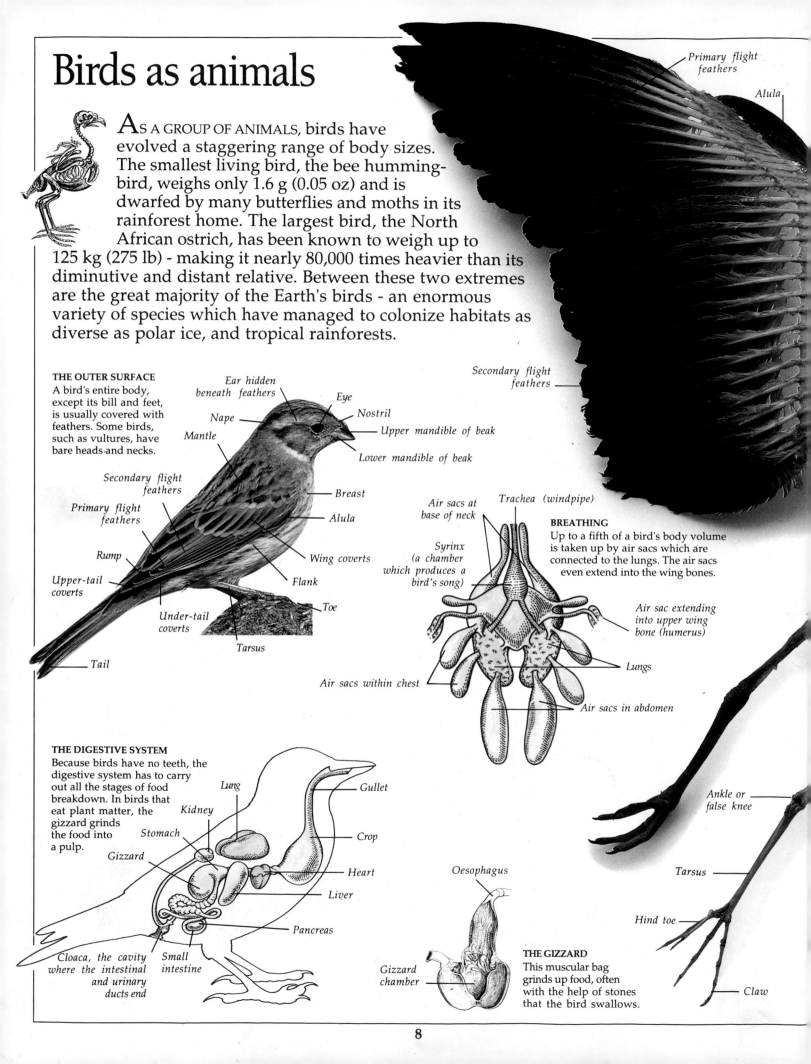

As a group of animals, birds have evolved a staggering range of body sizes. The smallest living bird, the bee hummingbird, weighs only 1.6 g (0.05 oz) and is dwarfed by many butterflies and moths in its rainforest home. The largest bird, the North African ostrich, has been known to weigh up to 125 kg (275 lb) - making it nearly 80,000 times heavier than its diminutive and distant relative. Between these two extremes are the great majority of the Earth's birds - an enormous variety of species which have managed to colonize habitats as diverse as polar ice, and tropical rainforests.

Primary flight feathers

Alula

Secondary flight feathers

THE OUTER SURFACE
A bird's entire body, except its bill and feet, is usually covered with feathers. Some birds, such as vultures, have bare heads and necks.

Ear hidden beneath feathers

Nape

Mantle

Eye

Nostril

Upper mandible of beak

Lower mandible of beak

Secondary flight feathers

Primary flight feathers

Breast

Alula

Rump

Wing coverts

Upper-tail coverts

Flank

Under-tail coverts

Toe

Tarsus

Tail

BREATHING
Up to a fifth of a bird's body volume is taken up by air sacs which are connected to the lungs. The air sacs even extend into the wing bones.

Air sacs at base of neck

Trachea (windpipe)

Syrinx (a chamber which produces a bird's song)

Air sac extending into upper wing bone (humerus)

Lungs

Air sacs within chest

Air sacs in abdomen

THE DIGESTIVE SYSTEM
Because birds have no teeth, the digestive system has to carry out all the stages of food breakdown. In birds that eat plant matter, the gizzard grinds the food into a pulp.

Lung

Kidney

Stomach

Gizzard

Gullet

Crop

Heart

Liver

Pancreas

Cloaca, the cavity where the intestinal and urinary ducts end

Small intestine

Oesophagus

Gizzard chamber

THE GIZZARD
This muscular bag grinds up food, often with the help of stones that the bird swallows.

Ankle or false knee

Tarsus

Hind toe

Claw

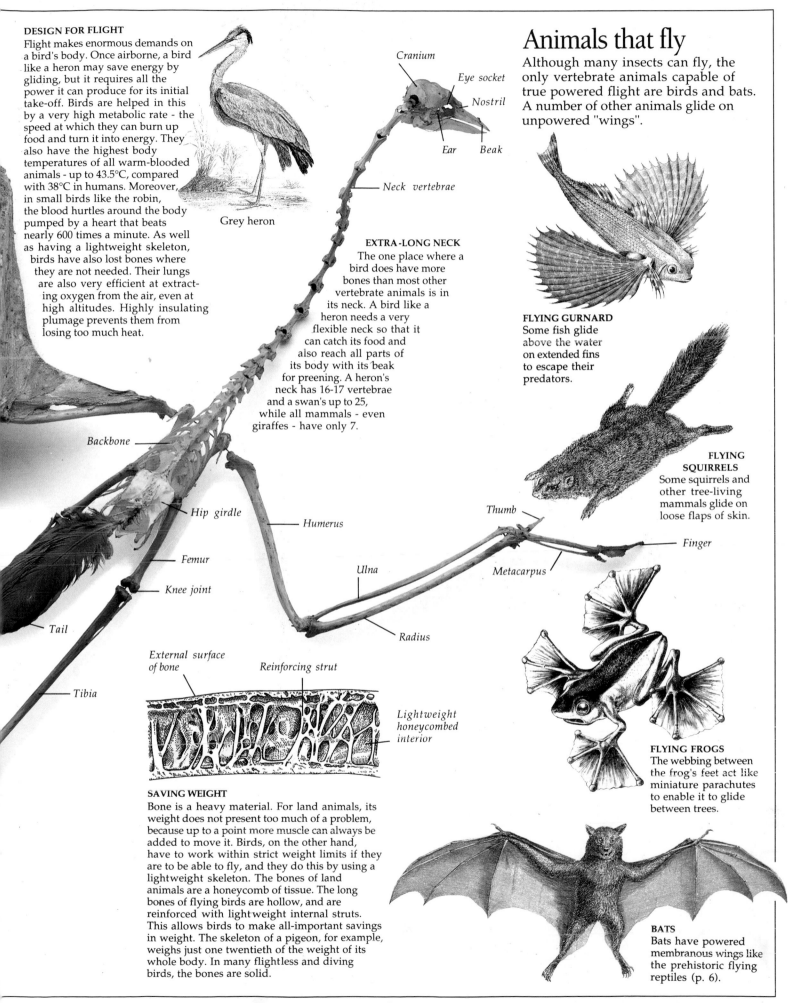

DESIGN FOR FLIGHT

Flight makes enormous demands on a bird's body. Once airborne, a bird like a heron may save energy by gliding, but it requires all the power it can produce for its initial take-off. Birds are helped in this by a very high metabolic rate - the speed at which they can burn up food and turn it into energy. They also have the highest body temperatures of all warm-blooded animals - up to 43.5°C, compared with 38°C in humans. Moreover, in small birds like the robin, the blood hurtles around the body pumped by a heart that beats nearly 600 times a minute. As well as having a lightweight skeleton, birds have also lost bones where they are not needed. Their lungs are also very efficient at extracting oxygen from the air, even at high altitudes. Highly insulating plumage prevents them from losing too much heat.

Grey heron

Cranium

Eye socket

Nostril

Ear   *Beak*

Neck vertebrae

EXTRA-LONG NECK

The one place where a bird does have more bones than most other vertebrate animals is in its neck. A bird like a heron needs a very flexible neck so that it can catch its food and also reach all parts of its body with its beak for preening. A heron's neck has 16-17 vertebrae and a swan's up to 25, while all mammals - even giraffes - have only 7.

Backbone

Hip girdle

Femur

Knee joint

Tail

Tibia

Humerus

Ulna

Radius

Thumb

Metacarpus

Finger

External surface of bone

Reinforcing strut

Lightweight honeycombed interior

SAVING WEIGHT

Bone is a heavy material. For land animals, its weight does not present too much of a problem, because up to a point more muscle can always be added to move it. Birds, on the other hand, have to work within strict weight limits if they are to be able to fly, and they do this by using a lightweight skeleton. The bones of land animals are a honeycomb of tissue. The long bones of flying birds are hollow, and are reinforced with lightweight internal struts. This allows birds to make all-important savings in weight. The skeleton of a pigeon, for example, weighs just one twentieth of the weight of its whole body. In many flightless and diving birds, the bones are solid.

Animals that fly

Although many insects can fly, the only vertebrate animals capable of true powered flight are birds and bats. A number of other animals glide on unpowered "wings".

FLYING GURNARD
Some fish glide above the water on extended fins to escape their predators.

FLYING SQUIRRELS
Some squirrels and other tree-living mammals glide on loose flaps of skin.

FLYING FROGS
The webbing between the frog's feet act like miniature parachutes to enable it to glide between trees.

BATS
Bats have powered membranous wings like the prehistoric flying reptiles (p. 6).

The wing

ONLY A FEW ANIMALS - the insects, bats and birds - are capable of powered flight, and of these three, the birds are by far the largest, fastest and most powerful fliers. The secret of their success lies in the design of their wings. A bird's wing is light, strong and flexible. It is also slightly curved from front to back, producing an "aerofoil" profile which literally pulls the bird upwards as it flaps through the air. Although the size and shape of wings vary according to a bird's individual lifestyle, all share the same pattern - shown here in the wing of an owl.

OVER THE LIMIT

A bird's wings can bear its weight, plus light luggage such as food and nesting materials. Heavier loads, like human passengers, are strictly out of the question.

FLIGHT OF FANCY

Legend has it that as Icarus flew from Crete to Greece, he climbed too near to the sun and the wax which held his feathers melted. But birds flying at high altitude have to cope with quite different and much more real problems - thin air, scarce oxygen and intense cold.

MECHANICAL MIMICRY

A brilliant anatomist, Leonardo da Vinci drew on his knowledge of bird wings to design machines that would imitate their flight. He replaced bones with wood, tendons with ropes, and feathers with sailcloth. As far as is known, none of these devices ever got beyond his drawing-board. They would have been far too heavy to fly.

FLAPPING FAILURES

The heroic birdmen of bygone days did not realize that flapping flight would always be beyond the power of human muscles. True man-powered flight has only been achieved through the later invention of the propeller.

ALULA

This group of feathers is held open in slow flight to prevent stalling.

PRIMARY FLIGHT FEATHERS

The "primaries" produce the power for flight as the bird brings its wings downwards. The outermost primaries can be used for steering, like the flaps on a plane's wing.

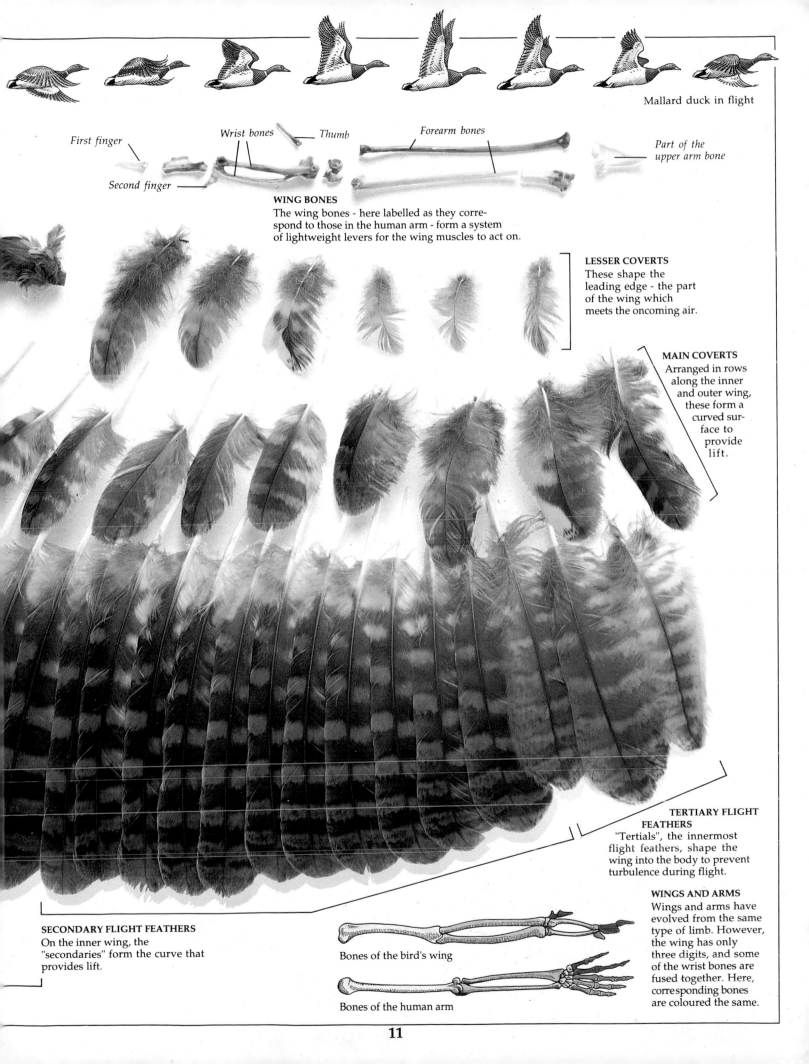

Mallard duck in flight

First finger

Second finger

Wrist bones   Thumb

Forearm bones

Part of the upper arm bone

WING BONES
The wing bones - here labelled as they correspond to those in the human arm - form a system of lightweight levers for the wing muscles to act on.

LESSER COVERTS
These shape the leading edge - the part of the wing which meets the oncoming air.

MAIN COVERTS
Arranged in rows along the inner and outer wing, these form a curved surface to provide lift.

TERTIARY FLIGHT FEATHERS
"Tertials", the innermost flight feathers, shape the wing into the body to prevent turbulence during flight.

WINGS AND ARMS
Wings and arms have evolved from the same type of limb. However, the wing has only three digits, and some of the wrist bones are fused together. Here, corresponding bones are coloured the same.

SECONDARY FLIGHT FEATHERS
On the inner wing, the "secondaries" form the curve that provides lift.

Bones of the bird's wing

Bones of the human arm

Manoeuvrability and fast take-off

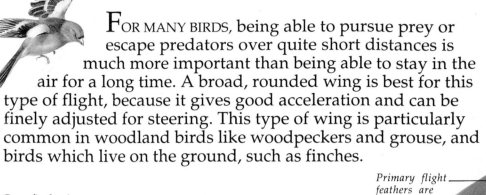

FOR MANY BIRDS, being able to pursue prey or escape predators over quite short distances is much more important than being able to stay in the air for a long time. A broad, rounded wing is best for this type of flight, because it gives good acceleration and can be finely adjusted for steering. This type of wing is particularly common in woodland birds like woodpeckers and grouse, and birds which live on the ground, such as finches.

OWL FLIGHT
The barn owl has a slow, buoyant flight.

Greenfinch wing

FINCH FLIGHT
Finches shut their wings periodically to save energy.

Broad wingtip

Primary flight feathers are curved and broad

QUICK ON THE TURN
The greenfinch's blunt, rounded wing shape is typical of finches. Except when migrating, finches rarely fly far, and constantly veer and turn on the wing. Flocking finches burst into the air at the least sign of danger.

Greenfinch

Owl wing coverts have a soft, downy texture

Fringed feather edges reduce air turbulence and cut down the noise produced by flight

Barn owl

MUFFLED WINGS
A barn owl's wing is almost furry to the touch. Its fringed feathers muffle the wingbeats so that small animals do not hear the owl's approach.

Roller wing

Broad flight feathers for manoeuvrability

Roller

Barn owl wing

PERCH TO PERCH
The roller, a bird about the size of a jay, catches small animals by swooping down onto them. It spots its prey from its perches on walls and trees, and it moves between perches with a slow, almost leisurely flight.

Light and dark barring camouflages bird when feeding on ground

Wing has a broad surface for manoeuvrability but a pointed tip for speed

READY TO ESCAPE
Most doves and pigeons are hunted by many predators, including man. Strong wing muscles (making up a third of its weight) enable them to take off rapidly and accelerate to 80 kph (50 mph).

Crested pigeon wing

ROLLER FLIGHT
The roller has a heavy up-and-down flight.

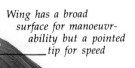

TURTLE DOVE FLIGHT
The wings beat rapidly without pauses.

Turtle dove

Woodpecker wing

WOODPECKER FLIGHT
Woodpeckers climb and dive much more steeply than most other birds.

Pheasants in flight

Green colouring for camouflage

Pheasant wing

Folded flight feathers

STEERING A SAFE COURSE
In tangled woodland, a green wood-pecker needs short, rounded wings so that it can turn suddenly to avoid obstacles. Its wing shape also helps it to come to a controlled landing when approaching a tree.

Woodpecker

Camouflaged inner wing feathers conceal bird on ground

Camouflaged plumage only found on the female

VERTICAL TAKE-OFF
Pheasants are reluctant fliers. If alarmed, they take off almost vertically on their broad wings. Once airborne, they then glide away in a straight line.

FLYING FOR COVER
Grouse, like pheasants and other game birds, spend most of their time on the ground. On sensing danger, they first crouch down. Then - waiting almost to the last moment - they spring upwards, at the same time bringing their opened wings sharply downwards, to burst into the air. Grouse fly by alternating rapid wingbeats with short glides, and only cover a short distance before landing. In nearly all game birds, the female's wings are camouflaged while the male's are more con-spicuous.

PHEASANT FLIGHT
Rapid wingbeats are followed by a long glide.

Female black grouse or "blackhen"

Female black grouse or "blackhen" wing

Long flight feathers allow the grouse to glide

Male black grouse or "blackcock" wing

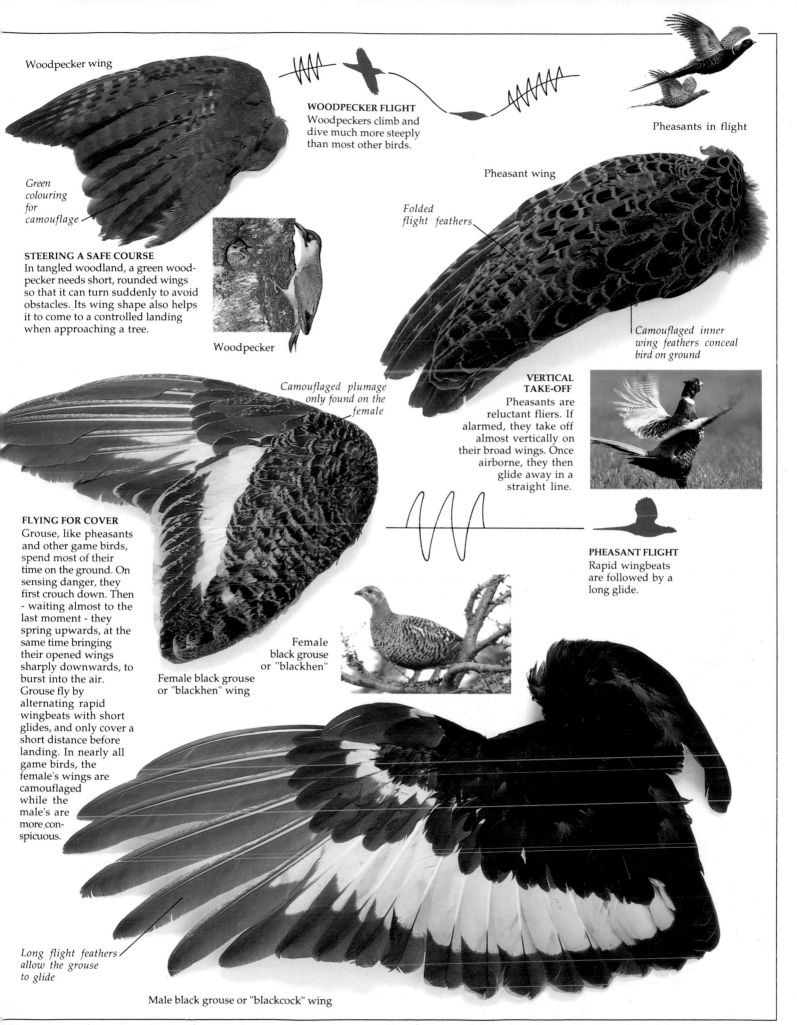

Speed and endurance

WHEN A SWIFT makes its first brief landing before nesting, it brings to an end a flight that may have lasted non-stop for three years. The swift is just one of a number of birds which only land to breed, and its slender curved wings are completely adapted for continuous use. In a similar way, the wings of all other birds have evolved for a particular kind of flight. In general, birds that fly rapidly and powerfully, like the swift, have pointed wings. This wing shape provides the bird with enough lift without producing too much drag. All the wings here are shaped for flapping flight, as opposed to soaring (p. 16).

Kingfisher wing

Waterproof flight feathers

Down feathers

SPEED IN BURSTS
The kingfisher's fast but short flight is achieved on stubby triangular wings. This wing shape helps the bird to take off from the water after a dive.

Kingfisher

KINGFISHER FLIGHT
Whirring wingbeats carry the kingfisher between perches. It can brake in mid-air to dive for fish.

Long outer wing feathers

Short inner wing feathers

Swift wing

NON-STOP FLIGHT
The swift's long, curved wings enable it to fly continuously at an average speed of about 40 kph (25 mph).

Swifts

SWIFT FLIGHT
The swift alternates fast wingbeats with short glides.

Wing coverts

Alula

Peregrine wing

Outer wing feathers are extended during level flight but closed up for diving

Long primary flight feathers

Inner wing feathers

Peregrine

Wing tip folds back when diving after prey

PEREGRINE FLIGHT
The peregrine falcon dives with its wings partially folded. This method of catching prey is known as "stooping".

SPEED RECORD-HOLDER
The peregrine falcon is the world's fastest bird. Although its speed is often exaggerated, it can probably dive at a breath-taking 280 kph (175 mph) in pursuit of other birds. As it dives, it slashes its victim with its talons, knocking it to the ground with the force of the impact.

LONG-HAUL MIGRANTS
Many geese travel enormous distances each year to breed in the Arctic tundra. Their flight is not particularly fast - they cruise at about 55 kph (35 mph) - but they are able to maintain this speed for many hours without stopping. Snow geese, for example, have been known to travel 2,700 km (1,700 miles) in two-and-a-half days. Goose wings are long and broad to provide the lift needed to keep birds weighing up to 5 kg (11 lb) airborne.

Lesser white-fronted goose

Primary flight feathers

Shoveler wing

Inner wing coverts

Speculum exposed during flight

Strong primary flight feathers

Shoveler

RAPID TRANSIT
Ducks like the shoveler migrate to breed, but their journeys are usually shorter than those of geese and their flight faster. A migrating duck can travel up to 1,600 km (1,000 miles) in a single day, averaging nearly 70 kph (40 mph). Many ducks have a brightly coloured patch, "speculum" on each wing, while others only develop them during the breeding season.

WATERFOWL FLIGHT
Both ducks and geese beat their wings constantly during flight.

Primary flight feathers

Speculum

Pointed tip of folded wing

Pintail wing

Broad wing surface gives maximum lift for take-off and long-distance flight

Pintail

WATERPROOF WINGS
The pintail, like most ducks, can escape from danger with a twisting and turning flight. It opens and closes its pointed wings to help it change direction. To keep its wings airworthy, the pintail waterproofs them with oil produced by a gland on its back and carefully preens them so that they lie in their correct position.

Lesser white-fronted goose wing

Soaring, gliding and hovering

WHEN A BIRD FLAPS ITS WINGS, it uses up a great deal of energy - about 15 times as much as when it is sitting still. But some birds have managed to evolve ways of flying that involve much less effort than this. Large birds do it by soaring and gliding - harnessing the power of the sun or the wind to keep them in the air. Right at the other extreme is hovering - keeping still in the air by beating the wings non-stop, just as a swimmer treads water to stay afloat.

Hummingbirds, the smallest flying birds, hover while feeding

Narrow wing provides lift without too much drag during gliding

Great black-backed gull wing

GLIDING GULLS
Slender, pointed wings enable gulls to glide on updraughts - currents of air deflected upwards by cliffs and hillsides. The lift generated by these updraughts is enough to support birds as heavy as the great black-backed gull, which weighs over 2 kg (4.5 lb).

Great black-backed gull

GULL FLIGHT
In flapping flight, a gull may travel at 40 kph (25 mph) while, in a strong updraught, it can stay motionless over the ground.

Inner wing coverts mould wing to the body

"Slotted" primary flight feathers reduce turbulence

Kestrel wing

HANGING IN THE AIR
Although many birds can hover momentarily, few can keep up this type of flight, as it is tremendously strenuous. One exception is the kestrel, which hovers as its keen eyes pinpoint shrews and voles from high overhead. It needs a slight headwind to help buoy it up.

Kestrel

KESTREL FLIGHT
The kestrel has the fluttering forward flight typical of falcons.

KESTREL HOVERING
The wings beat rapidly and the tail is fanned out to provide lift as the wind blows past it.

Birds that cannot fly

Millions of years ago, giant flightless birds roamed the Earth. Today, only a few dozen smaller species survive.

Penguin flipper

Stiff wing blade acts as a propeller

Densely packed feathers

Rhea wing

WINGS AS FLIPPERS
Penguins swim by "flying" underwater with their wings. One species, the emperor penguin, can dive up to 250 m (800 ft) using its wings for propulsion. Penguins' wings cannot be folded up like those of most birds.

Adelie penguins in Antarctica

Rhea

Inner wing

Downy feathers provide insulation but cannot produce lift

Outer wing

PAMPAS RUNNER
Rheas are the South American counterparts of ostriches. Their wing feathers are long, but useless for flight.

THE HEAVIEST BIRD
Ornithologists calculate that no bird heavier than 18 kg (40 lb) can be capable of flight because, above that weight, muscle power would never be sufficient to keep a bird airborne. The African ostrich, weighing in at 120 kg (260 lb), is nearly seven times over this limit. Its wings are no more than weak flaps that carry a fan of 16 fluffy flight feathers. Although the ostrich cannot fly, it can run at speeds of over 50 kph (30 mph).

Straight leading edge is held slanting upwards during soaring

Primary flight feathers are used for manoeuvering

Splayed "fingers" help to reduce air turbulence

Broad inner flight feathers provide lift as bird soars within a thermal

Buzzard wing

UP WITHOUT EFFORT
Heavy birds of prey like the buzzard soar on thermals - columns of warm rising air. They only need to use flapping flight to get from one thermal to the next.

Buzzard

BUZZARD FLIGHT
All soaring birds bank tightly to keep within the rising air of a thermal.

Tails

DURING the course of evolution, birds have gradually lost the part of the backbone that in other animals makes up the tail, and have replaced it with feathers. The size of these feathers is very variable. Some birds (such as guillemots and puffins) hardly have any tail at all, while others (such as peacocks and male birds of paradise) have tails that are so long that they make flight quite difficult.

Tail fanned on approach; body held horizontally

Landing; feet held forward to grasp perch

Tail closed as bird settles on perch

AIR BRAKE
When a bird comes in to land, it lowers and spreads out its tail feathers. The feathers act as a brake and slow the bird's approach.

Tips worn and frayed by flight

RUMP FEATHERS
Above the base of a woodpigeon's tail, the rump feathers provide insulation with their thick down.

Woodpigeon

TAIL COVERTS
Dense rows of these feathers lie over the base of the bird's tail and smooth the air flow over it.

TAIL FEATHERS
The woodpigeon, like most birds, has 12 tail feathers. The feather tips quite quickly become frayed through wear during flight.

Tail shapes

Flight puts many restrictions on a bird's shape. For this reason, birds that spend much of their time on the wing invariably have tails that are lightweight and streamlined. But other birds, especially those that live on the ground or in woodland, have been able to evolve tails that are shaped for uses other than flight. Some of these are used for balance, some for perching, and others for attracting the attention of a mate.

Rump feathers

Tail coverts

Rump feathers showing distinctive orange coloration, revealed during flight

Tail coverts

Crossbill tail

Fork to aid manoeuvrability

Elongated tail feathers

Magpie tail

Magpie

A TAIL FOR BALANCE

The central feathers in a magpie's tail are nearly 25 cm (10 in) long. Long tails are normally used for display, but because male and female magpies both have them, it is more likely that they are used for balance on the ground or when clambering in trees.

FORKED TAILS

In some birds, the central tail feathers are the longest. In others, particularly many of the finches, the situation is reversed to give the tail a forked shape. This arrangement probably gives small birds greater manoeuvrability.

Crossbill

Green woodpecker tail

Rump feathers

Great spotted woodpecker

Downy black-tipped rump feathers lying above tail coverts

Rump feathers

Tail coverts

Tail coverts

Tail coverts

Curved tail feathers used in display by male

Stiff quills

Sharp points created by abrasion of tail against trees

Great spotted woodpecker

Black grouse tail

TAILS FOR SUPPORT

A woodpecker uses its tail to brace itself as it climbs the trunk of a tree. Woodpecker tail feathers are unusually stiff so that they can support a large amount of the bird's weight. Being subjected to rather rough treatment, the tips of the feathers rapidly wear down.

Male pheasant with wing and tail feathers revealed during take-off

A TAIL FOR DISPLAY

The male black grouse has crescent-shaped tail feathers while the female's tail feathers are straight. Differences like this are a sure sign that the tail has evolved this shape for display rather than for flight.

Black grouse

Peacock

The structure of feathers

FEATHERS are the great evolutionary innovation that separates birds from all other animals. A hummingbird's plumage may number under 1,000 feathers, while a large bird like a swan may have over 25,000, with nearly four-fifths of these covering the head and neck alone. Like hair, claws and horns, feathers are made from a protein called keratin. It is this substance that gives them their great strength and flexibility. But for all their intricate structure, fully grown feathers are quite dead. As feathers develop, they split apart to form a complex mesh of interlinking filaments. Once this has happened, their blood supply is cut off. The feathers then serve their allotted time, unless lost by accident, and when worn out are finally discarded during moulting.

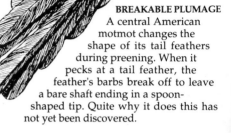

BREAKABLE PLUMAGE
A central American motmot changes the shape of its tail feathers during preening. When it pecks at a tail feather, the feather's barbs break off to leave a bare shaft ending in a spoon-shaped tip. Quite why it does this has not yet been discovered.

Feather sheaths

Emerging feather tufts

Growing feathers within sheaths

HOW FEATHERS GROW
Feathers start their growth as pulp inside tubes known as feather sheaths. The tip of a feather gradually begins to emerge from the growing sheath, unrolling and splitting apart to form a flat blade. Eventually the feather sheath falls away, leaving the fully formed feather.

FEATHER SHAFT
The hollow shaft contains the dried remains of the pulp.

Hollow interior

Pulp from interior of shaft

Fully grown feathers after the protective sheaths have fallen away

Quill tip embedded in skin and attached to muscles

MAN AND FEATHERS
Feathers have long been used by man for adornment and for more practical purposes. Head-dresses and quill pens both made use of flight feathers. The down feathers of ducks and geese are still collected for bedding, while the brilliantly coloured plumes of some tropical birds find their way into objects such as fishing flies.

Quill

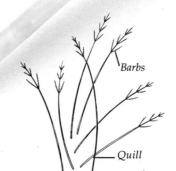

Barbs

Quill

FILOPLUMES
These hair-like growths, found between the feathers on a bird's body, help a bird to detect how its feathers are lying.

Aftershaft, second shaft from a single quill

SPLIT FEATHERS
Some feathers are split to form two different halves attached to the same shaft. This enables a single feather to perform two different functions.

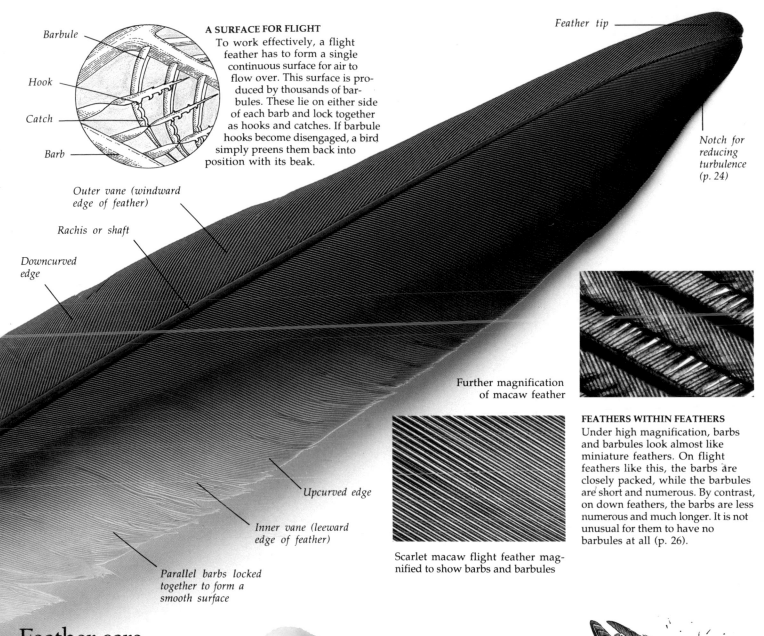

A SURFACE FOR FLIGHT
To work effectively, a flight feather has to form a single continuous surface for air to flow over. This surface is produced by thousands of barbules. These lie on either side of each barb and lock together as hooks and catches. If barbule hooks become disengaged, a bird simply preens them back into position with its beak.

Barbule

Hook

Catch

Barb

Feather tip

Notch for reducing turbulence (p. 24)

Outer vane (windward edge of feather)

Rachis or shaft

Downcurved edge

Upcurved edge

Inner vane (leeward edge of feather)

Parallel barbs locked together to form a smooth surface

Further magnification of macaw feather

FEATHERS WITHIN FEATHERS
Under high magnification, barbs and barbules look almost like miniature feathers. On flight feathers like this, the barbs are closely packed, while the barbules are short and numerous. By contrast, on down feathers, the barbs are less numerous and much longer. It is not unusual for them to have no barbules at all (p. 26).

Scarlet macaw flight feather magnified to show barbs and barbules

Feather care

Feathers receive a tremendous battering during daily use and, in addition, they easily become dirty and infested with parasites such as feather lice. Most feathers are shed every year during moulting, but nevertheless, birds have to spend much of their time ensuring that their plumage stays in an airworthy condition. They do this by preening - using the beak like a comb to draw together their feathers' barbs and barbules - and also by special methods of feather care, such as oiling, powdering and bathing, both in water and in dust.

POWDERED PLUMAGE
Egrets, herons and some other birds have special feathers which disintegrate to form a powder. This "powder down" is used to keep the plumage in good condition. Unlike other feathers, powder down feathers never stop growing.

ANTING JAYS
Jays sometimes encourage ants to swarm over their feathers. Poisonous formic acid produced by the ants may dislodge parasites in the jay's plumage.

DUST BATHS
Dust is both absorbent and abrasive. Bathing in dust cleans a bird's plumage by scouring dirt from the feathers.

Feathers

THE FEATHERS that make up a bird's plumage are of four main types - down feathers, body feathers and the feathers of the tail and wings. Although many of them are drab and unremarkable, others are beautifully shaped and coloured structures.

DOWN FEATHERS
Soft, finely divided feathers trap a layer of air to provide insulation.

Peacock

Pigeon

BODY FEATHERS
The feathers which stream-line a bird's body.

Macaw

African grey parrot

Red lory

Parrots

Macaws

TAIL FEATHERS
Feathers for steering, balance and display.

Goose

Goose

Flamingo

Peacock

Pheasants

Peacock

Palawan peacock pheasant

Golden pheasant

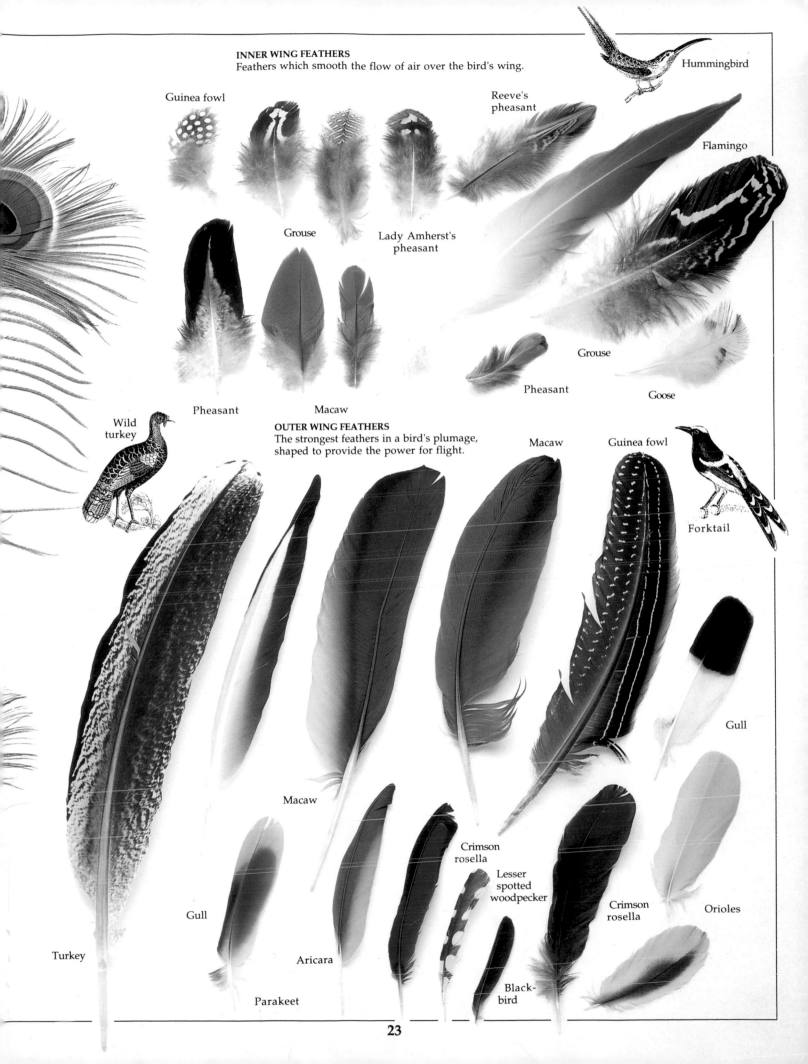

INNER WING FEATHERS
Feathers which smooth the flow of air over the bird's wing.

Guinea fowl

Reeve's pheasant

Hummingbird

Flamingo

Grouse

Lady Amherst's pheasant

Grouse

Pheasant

Goose

Pheasant

Macaw

Wild turkey

OUTER WING FEATHERS
The strongest feathers in a bird's plumage, shaped to provide the power for flight.

Macaw

Guinea fowl

Forktail

Gull

Macaw

Crimson rosella

Lesser spotted woodpecker

Crimson rosella

Orioles

Gull

Turkey

Aricara

Parakeet

Black-bird

Wing feathers

THE WING FEATHERS are one of the most important parts of a bird's flying machinery. They combine strength with lightness and flexibility. Compared with the rest of the body, the wings have relatively few feathers, but each one is important, working with its neighbours to form a perfect surface for flight.

The outer wing

The long feathers of the outer wing provide most of the bird's flight power and prevent it "stalling". The outermost flight feathers can be spread open or closed up in flight, thus helping a bird to steer.

Barn owl

Green woodpecker

Jay

Adult starling

Young starling

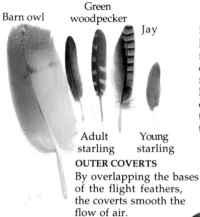

OUTER COVERTS
By overlapping the bases of the flight feathers, the coverts smooth the flow of air.

LOPSIDED DESIGN
Nearly all flight feathers are like this cockatiel's, being narrower on their leading edge. This design produces lift as the feather slices through the air.

GRADED SHAPES
Away from the wing tip, the flight feathers become progressively shorter and broader. These are from a regent parrot.

Fringe

Wider trailing edge

Slot

Narrow leading edge

Tawny owl

Barn owl

HEAVY-DUTY FEATHERS
The mute swan, which weighs up to 12 kg (26 lb), needs exceptionally long and strong feathers to power its flight. Its outer wing feathers can be up to 45 cm (18 in) long but, even so, each feather weighs only 15 g (0.5 oz).

ABOVE AND BELOW
Many wing feathers have differently coloured undersides. Macaws' feathers refract light to produce iridescent colours - in this species, blue above and yellow below.

SILENT FEATHERS
Fringes on the edges of owl feathers break up the flow of air and silence the owl's flight, as shown on this tawny owl feather.

SLOTTED FEATHERS
The deep slot in this crow feather forms a gap in the wing which reduces turbulence.

Swan

The inner wing

Inner wing feathers are generally shorter than those on the outer wing. They are not subject to so much force during flight and, for this reason, their quills are shorter and the feathers are less well anchored. With the exception of some display feathers, they are also more symmetrical than outer wing feathers.

A BALANCED BLADE
Inner wing feathers, here the regent parrot's, point away from the wind, not across it. They therefore do not need a lopsided shape to provide lift like the outer wing feathers.

IN-FLIGHT MARKINGS
The bright colours of many birds, such as budgerigars, are revealed only when the wings are fully open.

THE MANDARIN DUCK'S SAIL
The male mandarin duck has a pair of these extraordinary sail feathers - one at the base of each wing. They are shown off during courtship.

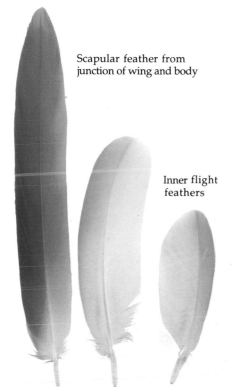

Scapular feather from junction of wing and body

Inner flight feathers

Curlew   Mallard   Jay

AT THE BOUNDARY
Flight feathers at the boundary between the inner and outer wing have curved quills and blunt tips. They may have bright patterning which shows up in flight.

CAMOUFLAGED FEATHERS
Patterned, brown feathers hide the woodcock from predators (p. 30).

COLOURED BY ITS FOOD
The greater flamingo lives on a diet of shrimps and other crustaceans. From these, it extracts a pink dye which becomes incorporated in its feathers.

Bustard

Rook

Curlew

Eagle owl

UNDERWING FEATHERS
Like the upperwing coverts, these lie close together to smooth the flow of air. The surface they produce is concave, rather than convex as in the upper wing.

INFREQUENT FLIERS
This feather is from a wild turkey. Like many birds that live on the ground, it rarely uses its feathers for flight.

INNER COVERTS
The inner coverts, in this case from a buzzard, overlap the front feathers of the inner wing. Their down shows that they are also used for insulating the body when the wing is folded.

own and tail feathers

...s are not only designed for
...hey also insulate and water-
pr... a bird's body, enable it to
conceal itself, attract a mate, incu-
bate its eggs, or stay balanced
when on the ground. All these tasks
are performed by three types of
feathers - body feathers, down feathers,
and the feathers in the tail. The way these
feathers work depends on their shape,
and whether or not their barbs
can lock together.

Down feathers

Down feathers are found
next to the bird's skin.
Their barbs do not lock
together, but instead
spread out to form a soft
irregular mass. Down is
one of the most effective
insulating materials found
in the animal kingdom.

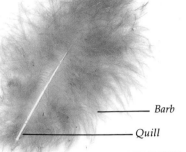

Barb

Quill

UNLOCKED BARBS
In this peacock down feather, the
separate barbs can be seen. These
barbs trap air which forms an insulation layer below the
body feathers.

THERMAL CLADDING
Small down feathers
like this one from a
partridge are packed
together tightly on the
bird's body to form a
fur-like mat.

**FEATHERS FOR
INCUBATION**
Many birds, including
the teal, pull out breast
feathers to insulate
their eggs. Some are
collected and sold for
bedding.

DUAL-FUNCTION FEATHER
Many feathers have a mass of down
near the point where they are
attached to the body, as shown on
this silver pheasant feather.

Body feathers

Body feathers come in a huge
range of shapes and sizes. Some
are used just to insulate and
cover the bird's body, but others
have developed a function for
display, and have evolved
bright colours or strange shapes.

Red lory
feathers

African grey
parrot feathers

Macaw feathers

PATTERNS ON THE SURFACE
In many boldly patterned birds, only the exposed
tips of the feathers show distinctive markings -
the rest of the feather is dull, as on this pheasant.

TROPICAL BRILLIANCE
Brilliant and varied body coloration is more common in birds that
live in the tropics than those that live in temperate regions. Bright
colours may help birds to identify their own kind among the
many others that share their habitat.

Long quill

COURTSHIP PLUMES
Some birds have evolved
body feathers that are completely adapted for a role in
attracting a mate. These
hanging feathers adorn
the neck of the male
wild turkey. Each
feather is divided
into a pair of
plumes.

FLYING HEAVYWEIGHT
This body feather comes
from a bustard - one of
the world's heaviest
flying birds.

LEAFY CAMOUFLAGE
The dull green tips of the
green woodpecker's body
feathers are ideal
camouflage against the
woodland leaves of its
natural habitat.

A PHEASANT'S CAPE
The neck feathers of the male golden
pheasant form a brilliant black and
gold cape. These feathers were once
highly sought-after by fishermen for
use in fishing flies.

Shortened barbs

Tail feathers

Birds use their tails for three things - to steer them during flight, to balance when perched or on the ground, and to impress a mate or a rival during courtship. Because of this, tail feathers come in a great range of shapes, sizes and colours, something which is particularly noticeable in breeding male birds.

A CURLED TAIL
The male mallard has two distinctive curled feathers at the base of its tail. When he courts a mate, he throws his head up and shows off his plumage. The female's tail feathers are straight.

EYED FEATHERS
The "eyes" on the peacock's tail extend right down to the short feathers at the tail's base, making a stupendous courtship display.

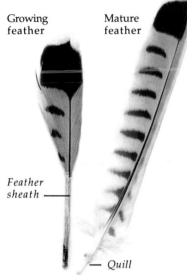

Growing feather

Mature feather

Feather sheath

— *Quill*

YOUNG AND OLD
Here, a growing tail feather from a kestrel is shown alongside a fully grown one. Both feathers are from a bird moulting into adult plumage.

STRESS BARS
The light-coloured bars in this parrot's tail feather are caused by changes in diet which occurred during the feather's growth.

BRED FOR COLOUR
Varied colours in budgerigars are the result of controlled breeding. Wild budgerigars are blue and green; other colours are only found in aviary birds.

THE TAIL'S SIDES
The feathers that are furthest from the centre of the tail are the least symmetrical because, when the tail is fanned in the air, the outer feathers must provide lift when air blows across them. These lopsided tail feathers are from a curlew.

CENTRAL TAIL FEATHER
This symmetrical owl feather comes from the centre of the tail.

IRIDESCENT TAILS
Magpies have long tail feathers that look black from a distance, but seem coloured when seen from nearby. As in the macaw's flight feathers (p. 24), this effect is caused by refraction.

GAME BIRD TAILS
The tails of male pheasants, chickens and other game birds can be exceptionally long. Even this long feather from a pheasant's tail would be completely dwarfed by that of a Japanese red jungle-fowl: its tail feathers have been bred to reach 10.5 m (35 ft).

Pheasant

Count Raggi's bird of paradise

Courtship

THE WAYS BY WHICH BIRDS FIND PARTNERS and mate is one of the most fascinating and colourful features of all animal life. Although divorce may be rare in birds, almost every other conceivable matrimonial arrangement exists somewhere in the bird world. Having fought off other males, often by establishing a territory, some males attract a single mate and remain faithful to her for life. At the other extreme, some males use their brilliant courtship plumage to attract a whole series of mates, deserting each one in favour of the next as soon as mating has taken place. Birds attract their mates by a combination of visible signals, which range from special plumage to brightly coloured legs and inflatable pouches, and by ritual movements, which vary from something as simple as a gull's nod of the head to the bizarre display in which the male great bustard throws back his wings and head, apparently turning his head inside out.

ROLE REVERSAL
Unusually for a bird, the female red phalarope courts the male. She is the more brightly coloured of the two birds.

THE PEACOCK'S TAIL
Peacocks are members of the pheasant family, a group of birds which show some of the most spectacular and elaborate courtship plumage in the bird world.

HIDDEN SUPPORT
From the back, the upright feathers of the peacock's "true" tail can be seen. These brace the much longer and more brilliant tail coverts.

ON PARADE
Male lyrebirds make themselves arenas on which they strut and display. Their posturing attracts a succession of mates.

Feathers without _____ barbules (p. 21) do not interlock, so appear lacy

_____ Tip of quill

A MYSTERY SOLVED

It was only in the last century that naturalists penetrated the forests of New Guinea and saw how plumes like this from a Count Raggi's bird of paradise were used by male birds. In displays, during which they hang upside down, the birds throw their plumes open.

Body feathers

Streaked central feather

During display, these feathers are thrown open to produce a fountain of colour as the male bird swings upside-down from a branch

INFLATABLE ATTRACTION

The male frigate bird has a brilliant red throat pouch which it uses to attract a mate. He keeps his pouch inflated for many hours until a female, lured by this irresistible courtship device, joins him.

DEFUSING TENSION

Although boobies and gannets nest in densely packed colonies, each bird will stab at any neighbour who dares to intrude on its small but very private "patch". When pairs meet, lengthy courtship ceremonies are needed to defuse these aggressive instincts. Here, two blue-footed boobies join in the "pelican" display, pointing their beaks out of each other's way.

IN STEP WITH THE SEASON

The brilliant colours on puffins' beaks are at their brightest during the breeding season in early summer. The colour lies in a horny sheath that covers the outside of the beak. When the puffins abandon their cliff-top burrows and head out to sea for the winter, this sheath falls off. The beak is then a much more subdued colour until the following spring.

DANCING ON WATER

Great crested grebes perform a sequence of bizarre dances during their courtship. The sequence often begins with a head-shaking dance, in which the birds face each other, jerking their heads from side to side, as if trying to avoid each other's glance. Suddenly, they dive and reappear at the surface with beakfuls of waterweed. During the "penguin dance" both birds rear up out of the water, paddling furiously as they present the weed to each other. After several more set-pieces, the birds mate.

MINIATURE RIVALS

Male hummingbirds, though tiny, pugnaciously defend their territories.

Camouflage

IN THE NATURAL WORLD, swaying reeds, beach pebbles, dead branches and patches of snow are not always what they seem. Any one of them can suddenly burst into life to reveal its true identity - a bird that only moments before was perfectly camouflaged against its background. When confronted by danger, most birds immediately take to the air. But some, particularly those that feed or roost on the ground, prefer to take a chance that they will be overlooked. The birds that lie low the longest are those with camouflaged plumage. In these, the colour and patterning of the feathers matches a particular kind of background, such as the woodland floor.

Woodcock

HIDDEN AMONG THE PEBBLES
An open beach may seem a difficult place for a bird to conceal itself. But the moment it stops moving, a ringed plover seems to vanish among the beach pebbles.

Ringed plover

THE FIRST LINE OF DEFENCE
The woodcock is a mainly nocturnal bird which lives in woodland. Between dusk and dawn it probes the woodland floor for worms and other small animals, but during the day it roosts on the ground. If its camouflage fails to conceal it, the woodcock will take off and dash through the tree trunks with a swerving flight.

Probing beak

Seasonal changes

On high mountain-sides and northern moorland, the winter snow completely changes the colour of the landscape. Birds that do not fly south for the winter need some way to hide from their enemies, and a few, like the ptarmigan (a type of grouse) do this by changing colour. Because birds moult their feathers every year, they can change their colour by shedding one set of feathers and replacing them with another, differently coloured set, which enables them to camouflage themselves. In places where the snow never melts, birds like the snowy owl have white plumage throughout the year.

Ptarmigan in winter plumage

Ptarmigan in summer plumage

SEASONAL PLUMAGE
In summer, the ptarmigan's feathers are brown enabling it to camouflage itself against rocks, but in the winter its plumage changes to white, thus concealing it effectively against snow.

Nightjar

A DAYTIME HIDEOUT
The nightjar is an insect-eater which feeds only at dusk. By day it stays completely still, looking like a broken branch. There are records of resting nightjars being trodden on by walkers who have not noticed birds right beneath their feet!

Feet and tracks

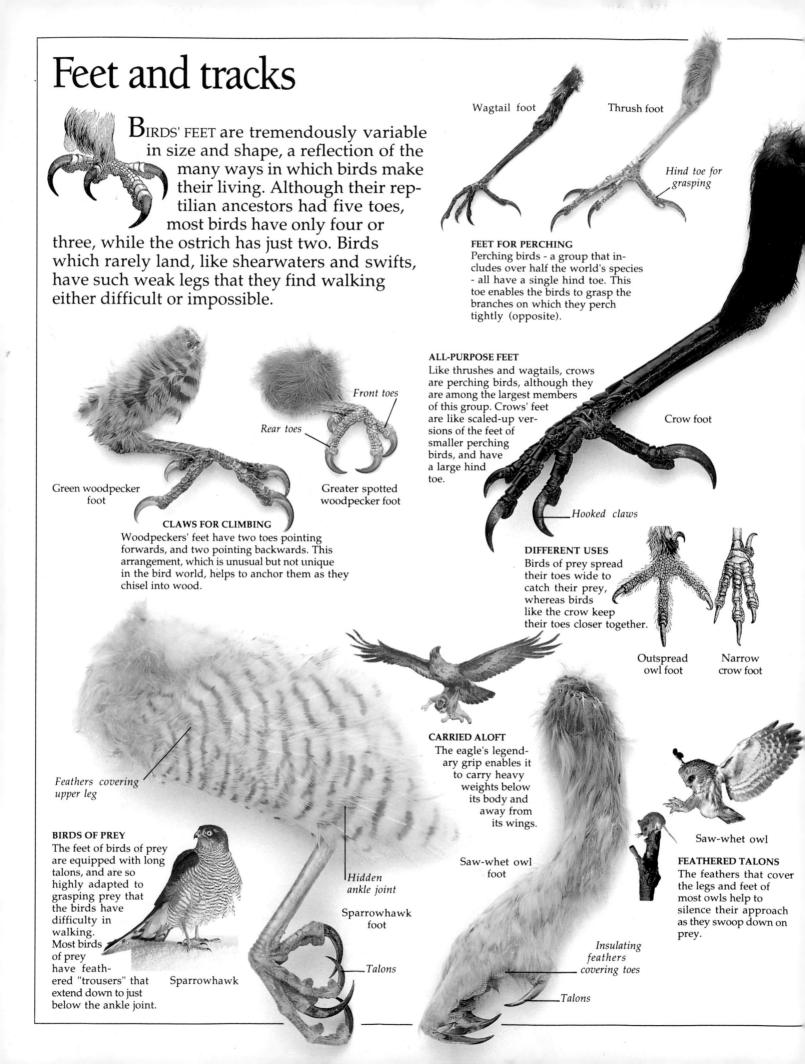

BIRDS' FEET are tremendously variable in size and shape, a reflection of the many ways in which birds make their living. Although their reptilian ancestors had five toes, most birds have only four or three, while the ostrich has just two. Birds which rarely land, like shearwaters and swifts, have such weak legs that they find walking either difficult or impossible.

Wagtail foot

Thrush foot

Hind toe for grasping

FEET FOR PERCHING
Perching birds - a group that includes over half the world's species - all have a single hind toe. This toe enables the birds to grasp the branches on which they perch tightly (opposite).

ALL-PURPOSE FEET
Like thrushes and wagtails, crows are perching birds, although they are among the largest members of this group. Crows' feet are like scaled-up versions of the feet of smaller perching birds, and have a large hind toe.

Crow foot

Front toes

Rear toes

Green woodpecker foot

Greater spotted woodpecker foot

CLAWS FOR CLIMBING
Woodpeckers' feet have two toes pointing forwards, and two pointing backwards. This arrangement, which is unusual but not unique in the bird world, helps to anchor them as they chisel into wood.

Hooked claws

DIFFERENT USES
Birds of prey spread their toes wide to catch their prey, whereas birds like the crow keep their toes closer together.

Outspread owl foot

Narrow crow foot

Feathers covering upper leg

CARRIED ALOFT
The eagle's legendary grip enables it to carry heavy weights below its body and away from its wings.

Saw-whet owl

BIRDS OF PREY
The feet of birds of prey are equipped with long talons, and are so highly adapted to grasping prey that the birds have difficulty in walking. Most birds of prey have feathered "trousers" that extend down to just below the ankle joint.

Sparrowhawk

Hidden ankle joint

Sparrowhawk foot

Talons

Saw-whet owl foot

FEATHERED TALONS
The feathers that cover the legs and feet of most owls help to silence their approach as they swoop down on prey.

Insulating feathers covering toes

Talons

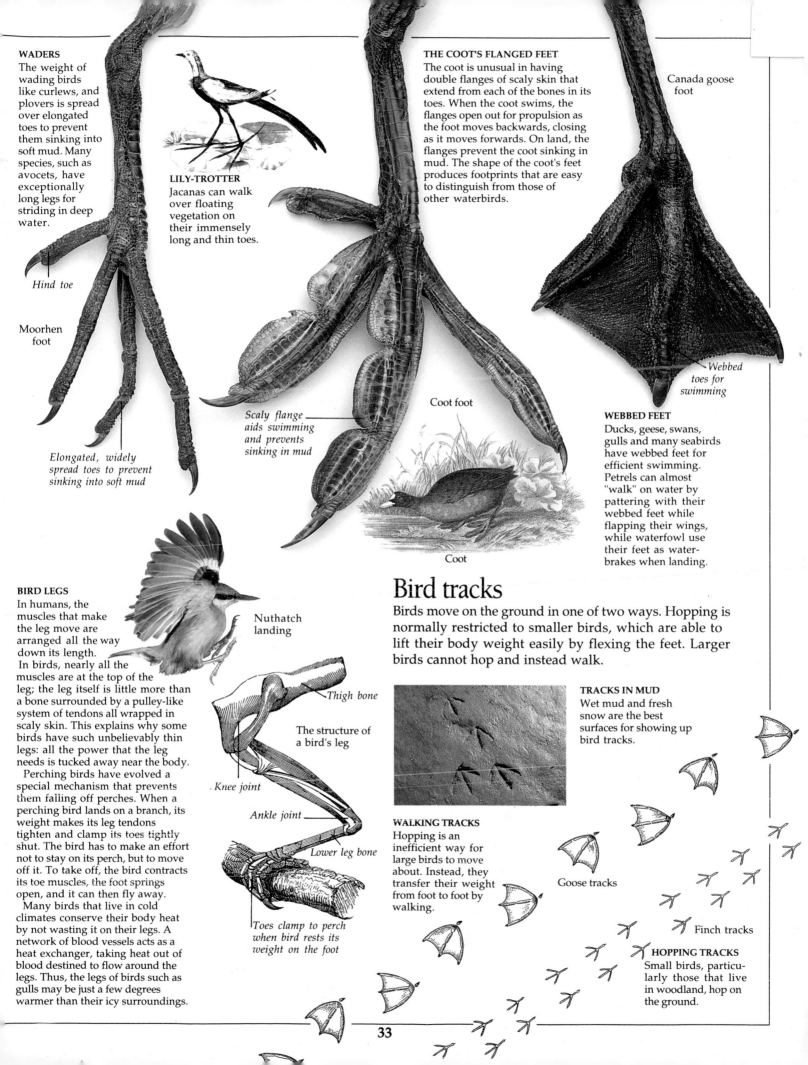

WADERS
The weight of wading birds like curlews, and plovers is spread over elongated toes to prevent them sinking into soft mud. Many species, such as avocets, have exceptionally long legs for striding in deep water.

Hind toe

Moorhen foot

Elongated, widely spread toes to prevent sinking into soft mud

LILY-TROTTER
Jacanas can walk over floating vegetation on their immensely long and thin toes.

THE COOT'S FLANGED FEET
The coot is unusual in having double flanges of scaly skin that extend from each of the bones in its toes. When the coot swims, the flanges open out for propulsion as the foot moves backwards, closing as it moves forwards. On land, the flanges prevent the coot sinking in mud. The shape of the coot's feet produces footprints that are easy to distinguish from those of other waterbirds.

Canada goose foot

Scaly flange aids swimming and prevents sinking in mud

Coot foot

Coot

Webbed toes for swimming

WEBBED FEET
Ducks, geese, swans, gulls and many seabirds have webbed feet for efficient swimming. Petrels can almost "walk" on water by pattering with their webbed feet while flapping their wings, while waterfowl use their feet as water-brakes when landing.

BIRD LEGS
In humans, the muscles that make the leg move are arranged all the way down its length. In birds, nearly all the muscles are at the top of the leg; the leg itself is little more than a bone surrounded by a pulley-like system of tendons all wrapped in scaly skin. This explains why some birds have such unbelievably thin legs: all the power that the leg needs is tucked away near the body.

Perching birds have evolved a special mechanism that prevents them falling off perches. When a perching bird lands on a branch, its weight makes its leg tendons tighten and clamp its toes tightly shut. The bird has to make an effort not to stay on its perch, but to move off it. To take off, the bird contracts its toe muscles, the foot springs open, and it can then fly away.

Many birds that live in cold climates conserve their body heat by not wasting it on their legs. A network of blood vessels acts as a heat exchanger, taking heat out of blood destined to flow around the legs. Thus, the legs of birds such as gulls may be just a few degrees warmer than their icy surroundings.

Nuthatch landing

Thigh bone

The structure of a bird's leg

Knee joint

Ankle joint

Lower leg bone

Toes clamp to perch when bird rests its weight on the foot

Bird tracks
Birds move on the ground in one of two ways. Hopping is normally restricted to smaller birds, which are able to lift their body weight easily by flexing the feet. Larger birds cannot hop and instead walk.

TRACKS IN MUD
Wet mud and fresh snow are the best surfaces for showing up bird tracks.

WALKING TRACKS
Hopping is an inefficient way for large birds to move about. Instead, they transfer their weight from foot to foot by walking.

Goose tracks

Finch tracks

HOPPING TRACKS
Small birds, particularly those that live in woodland, hop on the ground.

The senses

BIRDS LIVE IN A WORLD that is dominated by sight and sound. So important is their sense of vision that, for most birds, three of the other four senses - touch, smell and taste are largely irrelevant. A hovering kestrel sees very much greater detail in the ground below it than a human would at the same height but, having caught its prey, it is doubtful whether it can taste it. Whereas humans have thousands of taste buds on their tongues, most birds have less than a hundred. However, birds have good hearing. They can distinguish notes that are far too fast for humans to separate and one species, the oilbird of South America, can use sound to navigate just like a bat. But, with skulls packed with such sensitive eyes and ears, birds have not evolved large brains.

Members of the crow family, such as the raven, are the acknowledged intellectuals of the bird world

Raven skull

Separate bones in the cranium are fused together into a lightweight, but strong, protective case

Cranium

Nostril cavity connects with small paired nostrils that lie just behind the horny sheath of the beak

Opening to internal ear, usually hidden by a thin layer of short feathers

Eye socket points sideways in nearly all birds except those that catch fast-moving prey such as mammals and fish

Jugal bone at base of eye socket supports a bird's large eyes

SENSES AND THE SKULL
Like all parts of its body, the skull of the raven is modified to make it light enough for flying. In most animals, the separate bony plates that make up the cranium meet at long complicated joints called sutures. In a bird's cranium, the separate bones are fused together for extra strength, allowing the bones themselves to be thinner. The eyes are often bigger than the brain, and are kept in their sockets by a ring of tiny bones attached to the bird's eyeball.

INTELLIGENCE AND INSTINCT
Birds' brains are small compared to those of mammals, and most birds are poor at learning new skills. However, a bird is born with a huge number of "programmes" built into its brain. These programmes control not only simple activities like preening and feeding, but also feats of instinct such as migration.

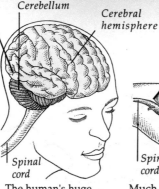

Optic lobe
Cerebellum
Cerebral hemisphere
Spinal cord

The human's huge cerebral hemisphere allows rapid learning

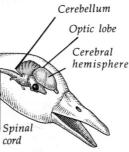

Cerebellum
Optic lobe
Cerebral hemisphere
Spinal cord

Much of the bird's brain is concerned with visual information

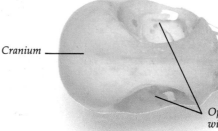

Cranium

Opposed eyes for wide-angle vision

Snipe skull

Bird vision

The eyes of owls point almost directly forward, giving a wide field of binocular vision. This arrangement enables owls to assess distance very accurately, and it is shared by nearly all hunting birds. Birds that are themselves hunted tend to have eyes that point in opposite directions. The woodcock, for example, can see all around and above itself without moving its head. Most other birds' vision lies between these two extremes.

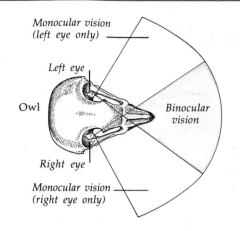

Monocular vision (left eye only)

Left eye

Owl

Right eye

Binocular vision

Monocular vision (right eye only)

REAR VIEW
Birds cannot swivel their eyeballs nearly as far as most other animals. An owl's eye movement, for example, is under two degrees, compared with 100 degrees for a human. Birds make up for this by having very flexible necks which can be turned to point backwards.

Woodcock

Left eye

Monocular vision (left eye only)

Forward binocular vision

Blind spot

Right eye

Monocular vision (right eye only)

Rear binocular vision field enables bird to see predators approaching from behind

HUNTING IN DARKNESS
Some owls are able to hunt in complete darkness, using their ears to locate the sounds made by a scurrying animal.

Higher ear cavity

Lower ear cavity

The unusual arrangement of an owl's ears is usually masked by its feathers

THE OWL'S UNBALANCED EARS
Owls hunt by night, when levels of light and sound are very low. For this reason, an owl needs not only very acute vision, but also extremely good hearing. Owls do not have external ears (although some species have ear-like tufts of feathers), but their broad faces gather sound-waves in just the same way as an external ear and direct them to the ear-drum within the skull. Owls' left and right ears are often at different levels in the skull. Each ear catches a sound at a slightly different time, giving improved "binaural" hearing which the owl uses to pinpoint its prey.

Hooked beak

Cranium

Ear

Forward-pointing eye socket for binocular vision

Owl skull

SENSITIVE BEAKS
Like other animals, birds feel with sensitive receptors which are attached to nerves. These receptors are scattered all over the body but, in long-billed birds, they also occur on the tip of the beak. When a wading bird probes into deep mud with its beak, it can actually feel what is below it.

Snipe

Elongated upper and lower mandibles of beak enable the snipe to reach food buried in mud

Sensitive tip of beak detects buried animals

FEELING FOR FOOD
Nightjars have bristles which extend forwards from either side of their mouths. These are extremely fine barbless feathers, and are probably used to funnel flying insects into the bird's mouth. Although birds do not have sensory hairs such as whiskers, it is possible that the nightjar can use its bristles to feel food.

Beaks

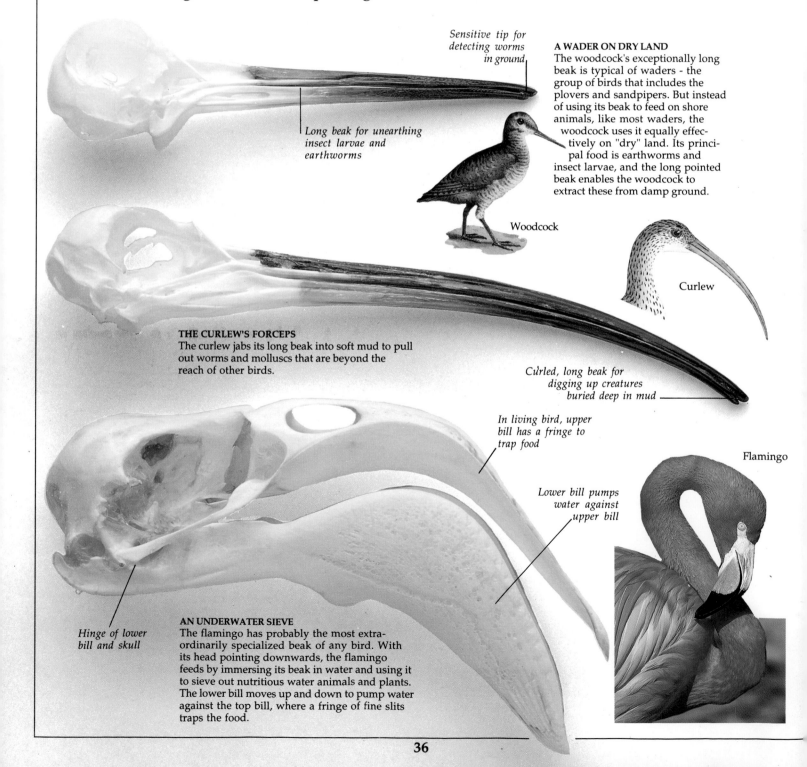

BECAUSE THEIR FRONT LIMBS are completely adapted for flight, most birds - with the important exception of birds of prey and parrots - catch and hold their food with their beaks alone. Birds' beaks have evolved a great variety of specialized shapes to enable them to tackle different kinds of food. This specialization was shown until recently by the huia of New Zealand. In this remarkable species, sadly now extinct, the male's beak was short and straight for probing, while the female's was long and curved for picking out insects.

Cone-shaped beak   Chaffinch

THE SEED-CRACKER
A bird's beak produces the greatest force nearest its base. Birds like chaffinches, which live on hard seeds, have short cone-shaped beaks so that they can crack open their food with as much force as possible. Finches deftly remove the cases of seeds with their beaks before swallowing them.

Sensitive tip for detecting worms in ground

Long beak for unearthing insect larvae and earthworms

A WADER ON DRY LAND
The woodcock's exceptionally long beak is typical of waders - the group of birds that includes the plovers and sandpipers. But instead of using its beak to feed on shore animals, like most waders, the woodcock uses it equally effectively on "dry" land. Its principal food is earthworms and insect larvae, and the long pointed beak enables the woodcock to extract these from damp ground.

Woodcock

Curlew

THE CURLEW'S FORCEPS
The curlew jabs its long beak into soft mud to pull out worms and molluscs that are beyond the reach of other birds.

Curled, long beak for digging up creatures buried deep in mud

In living bird, upper bill has a fringe to trap food

Flamingo

Lower bill pumps water against upper bill

Hinge of lower bill and skull

AN UNDERWATER SIEVE
The flamingo has probably the most extraordinarily specialized beak of any bird. With its head pointing downwards, the flamingo feeds by immersing its beak in water and using it to sieve out nutritious water animals and plants. The lower bill moves up and down to pump water against the top bill, where a fringe of fine slits traps the food.

Kestrel

A MEAT-EATER'S BEAK
The kestrel has a hooked beak typical of falcons and other birds of prey. The hook enables these meat-eating birds to pull apart animals which are too big to be swallowed whole.

Hook

Medium-length pointed beak for seeds and larger food

Blackbird

A TWEEZER BEAK
The blackbird has a beak shape that is shared by thousands of species of medium-sized birds. It is sharply pointed to allow the bird to pick up small objects like seeds, but its length allows the bird to grasp larger food items such as earthworms. The male blackbird's orange-yellow beak is also used as a signal to female birds.

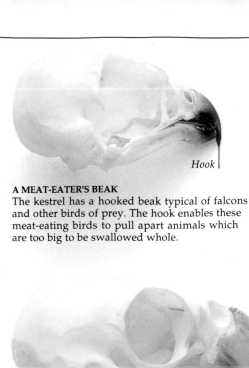

Parrot

Nostril

Area where seeds are cracked open

Hook for grasping fruit

A FRUIT-EATER'S BEAK
Wild parrots live on fruit and seeds and they have a "combination" beak to allow them to make the most of their food. A parrot uses the hook at the beak's tip to pull at the pulp of fruit, while it uses the jaws near the base of the beak to crack open the seeds and reach the kernels. Parrots are unusual in the bird world in the way they also use their feet to hold and turn their food while they crack it open.

Teeth for catching fish, made out of the horny material of the beak

A BEAK FOR DABBLING
Many ducks feed by "dabbling" or opening and shutting the beak while skimming it across the water's surface. Water enters the two flattened halves of the beak, and then anything suspended in it is strained out and swallowed. A duck's dabbling is rather like the sieving action of a flamingo, although a duck's beak is much less specialized and can be used for other kinds of feeding.

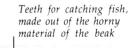

A DUCK WITH "TEETH"
Unlike mammals and reptiles, birds do not have true teeth, which are made of bone. However, some birds have evolved structures which are very like teeth. The mergansers, for example, have tooth-like serrations on the sides of their beaks. They use these beak teeth to catch fish, both in fresh water and out at sea.

Merganser

Flattened beak

Long, hooked beak for catching fish and ripping them apart

Scoter

ALL-PURPOSE BEAK
Gull's beaks are long and end in a hook which is smaller but in many ways similar to that of meat-eating birds. This beak shape not only enables a gull to catch and hold prey like fish along the length of the beak, it also enables them to pull apart their food.

Gull

Plant- and invertebrate-eaters

THE WORLD'S MOST NUMEROUS wild bird, the red-billed quelea, is a seed-eater. Over one hundred billion of these birds scour African fields and grassland for food, forming flocks that are millions strong. Birds like the quelea can survive in huge numbers because they live on a food that is incredibly abundant. Seeds, grass, nectar, insects, worms and many other small animals exist in prodigious quantities, and together they form the food for the majority of the world's birds.

Thrush

Eating plants and seeds

Birds that eat plants and seeds have to crush their food before they can digest it. As they have no teeth, they do this with powerful beaks and also with the gizzard (p. 8) - a muscular "grinding chamber" in their stomachs.

Finch skull

Hard-cased seeds

Goose skull

SPECIALIST SEED-EATERS
Finches, which number over 150 species, have short, sharp bills for breaking open seeds and nuts. Amazingly, some finches have bills which can exert more crushing force than a human hand.

Leaf crops

Cultivated grain

Pigeon skull

FEEDING ON CROPS
Pigeons and doves originally ate the leaves and seeds of wild plants: now they often feed on cultivated ones as well. They can also use their pointed bills like a straw when drinking - a unique ability among birds.

LIVING ON GRASS
Geese are among the few kinds of birds that can live on a diet of grass. But geese digest grass poorly, and it passes through their bodies in just two hours. Because they get so little out of their food, they must eat a lot of it, and so feed almost constantly.

Broad bill for tearing grass

Capercaillie skull

Powerful hooked beak for grasping leaves from trees and crushing seeds

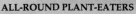

ALL-ROUND PLANT-EATERS
Game birds - species like pheasants, grouse and this capercaillie from Northern Europe - eat whatever plant food is available, although their preference is for seeds. In winter, the capercaillie lives on the leaves of coniferous trees, a source of food which few other animals use. It pulls the leaves from branches with its powerful hooked beak.

Seeds

Needles of conifer trees

The grass and waterplants on which geese feed

Invertebrate-eaters

Every spring, the number of insects and other invertebrates (animals without backbones) increases dramatically. These animals form the food for dozens of species of migratory birds. In winter, the supply is much smaller and food is harder to find, consisting mainly of larvae (grubs) in wood or in the soil. These are sought out by specialist insect-eaters.

Blackcap skull

Aphids

Caterpillar

PROBING WARBLERS
These small songsters use their probing beaks to pick insects from leaves and bark. When the supply dries up in early autumn, they migrate southwards.

THE SNAIL-SMASHER
Thrushes eat a wide range of food - both plant and animal. Some feed on snails, which they smash open on stone "anvils".

Thrush skull

Snail shells broken open by thrush

Earthworms are eaten not only by garden birds, but also by some owls and even birds of prey

Pecked apple

Woodpecker skull

Centipede

Beetle larvae

Adult beetle

Hoopoe skull

LARGE INSECT-EATERS
Birds like woodpeckers and the mainly ground-feeding hoopoe use their beaks to pick large insects out of crevices in trees. Woodpeckers also chisel into the wood to find concealed grubs. Their extremely long tongues have spear-like tips which are used for impaling their prey.

Feeding on the shore

Although there are very few salt-water insects, the seashore contains a year-round supply of other invertebrates for birds to eat, from crabs and shellfish to burrowing worms.

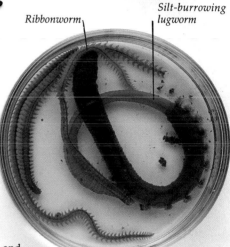

Avocet feeding

Ribbonworm

Silt-burrowing lugworm

Avocet skull

THE SWEEP-NET BEAK
The avocet catches worms and other prey by striding forward and sweeping its beak from side to side. It is one of the very few birds with an upturned beak.

Worms

Crab broken open and eaten; the hard skeleton is usually discarded

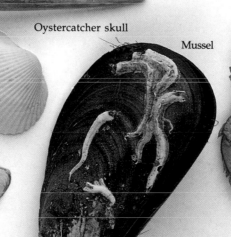

Oystercatcher skull

Mussel

A BUILT-IN HAMMER
The oystercatcher feeds on seashore animals with hard shells. It has a long beak like the avocet but, instead of ending in a fine point, its tip is blunt. This "built-in hammer" enables the oystercatcher to smash through the shells of its prey. This kind of feeding needs considerable skill, and some oystercatchers prize shells open instead. An experienced bird will know precisely where the weak points are on a mussel or cockle's shell and, if it is lying on sand, the bird will carry the shell to a rock to break it open.

Cockles

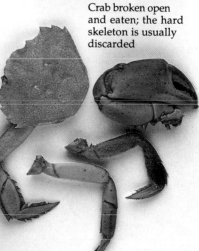

Hunters, fishers and all-rounders

FLIGHT ENABLES BIRDS to cover great distances in search of food. This gives them a great advantage as predators, because few animals - on land or far out at sea - are beyond their reach. Flight also makes birds very effective all-round feeders. A dead animal, an unprotected nest or a field of ripening crops is quickly spotted by passing birds and turned into a satisfying meal.

Kingfishers

Meat-and fish-eaters

Birds that feed on larger animals and fish catch their prey in two different ways. Most fish-eaters use their beaks to catch their quarry while, on land, birds of prey use their talons for catching and their beaks for tearing.

Strips of meat torn from prey with powerful, hooked beak

Tawny owl skull

Fur is swallowed and later discarded in pellets

NIGHT AND DAY HUNTERS

In general, owls and birds of prey such as the buzzard operate like two sets of shift workers, catching rodents and larger mammals around the clock. A few owls do hunt by day, but no bird of prey can hunt during the night.

Buzzard skull

Large forward-pointing eyes enable the gannet to pinpoint fish below

Halves of the beak meet at a long straight line for holding fish before they are swallowed

Streamlined point for diving

Gannet skull

ABOVE AND BELOW WATER

Gannets dive-bomb shoals of fish by plunging, with their wings folded, from heights of up to 30 m (100 ft). They stay below the surface for only a few seconds. Cormorants pursue fish underwater. Their feathers do not trap air like other waterbirds, and this enables them to dive swiftly and overtake their prey.

PATIENCE REWARDED

The heron fishes by stealth, staying motionless until its prey swims within reach of its long stabbing beak.

Hooked beak for grasping fish

Cormorant skull

Mackerel

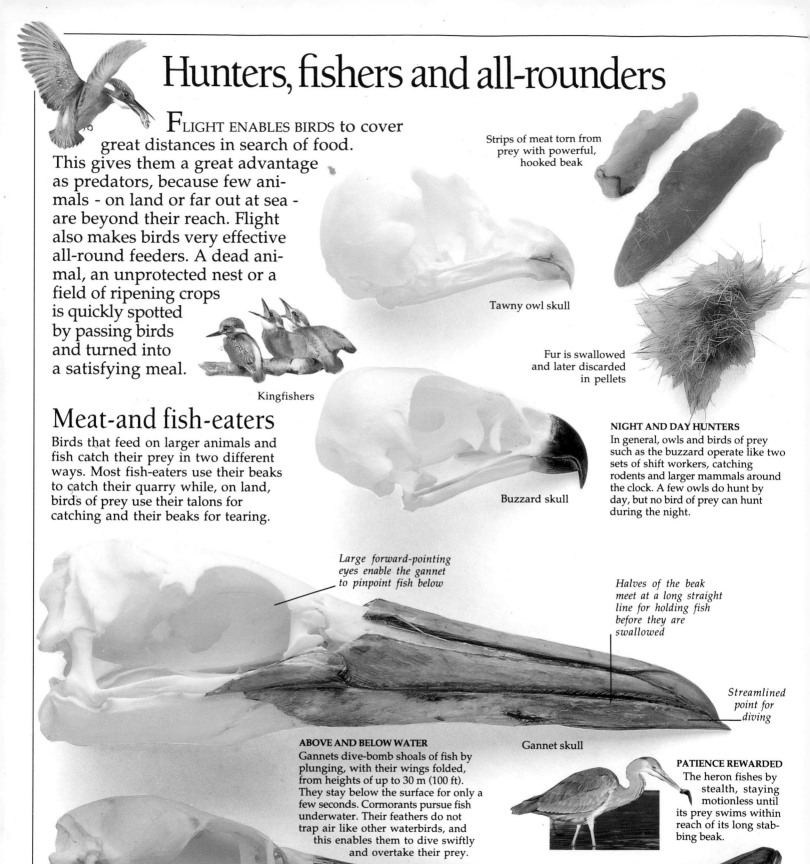

40

A mixed diet

It doesn't take much intelligence to be a successful seed-eater, but birds that survive on a mixed diet must live on their wits. These scavengers are quick to take a chance which might lead to a meal, where other birds would hesitate and miss out. They thrive on waste food and household rubbish, as well as more natural food items.

Crows eat all kinds of animal remains and are particularly adept at finding animal casualties on roads

Seeds from fields and farmyards

METAL MEALS
Ostriches are famed for their scavenging. They have even been known to eat metal, sometimes with fatal results.

Magpie skull

Ground beetle

Centipede

Insects and invertebrates, usually swallowed whole and partially regurgitated in pellets (p. 42)

Egg broken open after being stolen from nest

Crow skull

Jay skull

Earthworm

EVER-ADAPTABLE CROWS
The members of the crow family are among the most successful general feeders in the bird world. There are few places where they cannot be found. One of the reasons for their success is their inquisitive nature, which is backed up by boldness and a strong, all-purpose beak. Insects, dead birds, live mammals, worms and seeds all feature on their menu, while anything that cannot be eaten may well be carried off for further inspection.

Nuts eaten by birds have rough-edged holes; those eaten by rodents show small teeth marks

Broad-bodied libellula dragonfly larva

Toad tadpole

Duckweed

Ramshorn water snail

Greater pondsnail

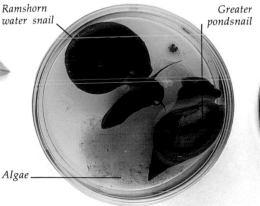

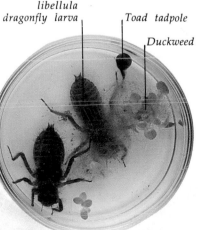

Coot skull

A FRESHWATER OPPORTUNIST
The coot is a small aggressive bird of lakes and rivers. It eats any water life that it can find - this can include not only waterweed, snails, tadpoles and fish, but also young birds. Young ducklings are particularly at risk from the coot's attacks.

Algae

Water snails from slow-moving fresh water

Animals and plants eaten by coots in shallow ponds

Pellets

PREDATORY BIRDS like owls feed on small mammals and birds but, because they do not have teeth, they cannot chew their food. Instead, they either rip their prey apart with their claws or eat it whole. This means that they swallow large quantities of bones, fur and feathers, which they cannot digest. So once or twice a day they regurgitate these items, packed tightly together, as pellets. The shape of a pellet identifies the species of bird that produced it, while the contents of the pellet show what the bird has been eating.

PELLETS IN OPEN GROUND
The short-eared owl hunts in daylight over rough grassland and marshes, catching voles and sometimes young birds. Its pellets are cylindrical with rounded ends. This particular species of owl does not drop its pellets from a perch, but scatters them around low tussocks of grass.

Rounded ends

Limb bone from a rodent

Blunt ends

Smooth dark crust

PELLETS BENEATH A ROOST
The smooth, almost black pellets of the barn owl are easy to identify. They often accumulate in small piles beneath roosts in barns and other old buildings.

Recent pellet still in compact state

Older pellet beginning to disintegrate

Protruding bones, typical of tawny owl pellets

Earth and fur

Pointed ends

Beetle wing-case

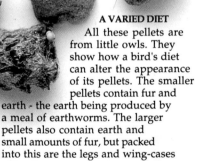

A VARIED DIET
All these pellets are from little owls. They show how a bird's diet can alter the appearance of its pellets. The smaller pellets contain fur and earth - the earth being produced by a meal of earthworms. The larger pellets also contain earth and small amounts of fur, but packed into this are the legs and wing-cases of beetles.

Beetle leg

PELLETS IN PARKS AND GARDENS
Tawny owl pellets are the only ones commonly found in parks - where it often nests - in suburbs and also in the countryside. Tawny owls eat voles, mice, shrews and birds, as well as much smaller animals. Their pellets are smooth and sometimes have pointed ends. Pellets that have been on the ground for a while often crumble to reveal a mass of protruding bones and tangled fur.

Shell fragments

Wing-cases of beetles mixed in with plant material

Seeds left behind after the soft flesh of berries has been digested

Rodent limb bone

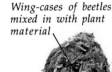

Seed-cases mixed with shell fragments

Metal foil

Fur

WADER PELLETS
The curlew and many other wading birds eat hard-shelled animals such as crabs. Their pellets contain fragments of these shells, sometimes mixed with the cases of seeds.

CROW PELLETS
Crows and their relatives eat all kinds of food. Their pellets often contain insect remains and plant stalks.

SONGBIRD PELLETS
Thrushes and blackbirds produce pellets that contain seeds. This specimen also contains a small piece of metal foil.

FALCON PELLETS
Birds like the kestrel and peregrine falcon produce pellets that contain bird, mammal and insect remains.

Inside an owl pellet

By pulling apart a pellet, it is possible to find out something about an owl's diet. Here, two tawny owl pellets have been carefully taken apart. The first pellet shows that the owl that produced it had dined entirely on voles - three of these small mammals made up the bird's nightly catch. The second pellet tells a rather different and more surprising story.

COMPLETE PELLET
When the pellet is dry, the fur and bones are matted together.

Fur, mixed with mucus, forms the "glue" that binds the pellet together

Rodents can be identified by the shape of their cheek-teeth; these are from a vole

Three vole skulls, two still intact

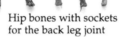

Ball joint on leg bone fits into this socket

Hip bones with sockets for the back leg joint

Bones from front limbs

Shoulder blades which attach to the front legs

Cheek-teeth

Complete jaw

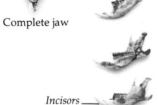

Incisors

The two sides of the jaw often break apart in the owl's stomach and they usually become separated from the skull

Leg bones, some still paired as they would have been in life

Curved ribs with flattened sides

Vertebrae - the distinctive bones which make up the backbone

FEEDING ON OTHER BIRDS

Although owls are often thought of as living on rodents and nothing else, these starling bones show that birds are very much a feature of the tawny owl's diet. Amazingly, the owl has managed to swallow and regurgitate the starling's large skull almost intact. Feathers, like fur and claws, are made of an indigestible protein, and have to be disposed of along with the bones.

Starling skull

Lower half of beak

Vertebrae from the starling's backbone

Wishbone (part of the shoulder)

Leg with complete claw still attached

Foot

Claw

Swallowed body feathers

Flight feathers - some with quills that have snapped in two

Leg and wing bones

Ribs

Making a nest

NEST-BUILDING is a job with two parts that run in tandem - collecting the materials and fashioning them into the finished nest. The amount of time spent in collecting depends on how far away the materials are: a reed-warbler hardly has to move to find dry reed leaves, whereas a swallow must find a puddle that will provide exactly the kind of mud that it needs. Birds go through a special sequence of movements to work materials into their nests. When a cup-nester returns to the nest with materials, it first pushes them roughly into place. The bird then sits in the centre of the nest and begins to turn around and around, pushing downwards and outwards with its breast. This circular movement, which gives the inside of the nest its shape, is shared by all birds. Cup-nesters turn and push, while birds such as herons turn and trample, pulling at individual sticks on the nest platform as they do so.

NATURAL MATERIALS

Nest materials have two main functions - support and insulation. Most hedgerow and woodland birds use sticks for the main structure of their nests, adding an insulating lining which may be of feathers, seed heads or animal fur. House martins and some swallows make their nests entirely out of mud, while another insect-eater, the swift, collects nesting material in mid-air by catching floating fibres in its beak.

MUD
Mixed with saliva to form a sticky paste.

SEED HEADS
Used in the nest lining for insulation.

LEAVES AND NEEDLES
Used for the inside of many cup nests.

TWIGS AND STICKS
Main structural material in larger nests.

MAN-MADE MATERIALS

Anything that can be carried away may end up in a bird's nest. Pigeons have been found nesting, quite literally, on beds of nails, and coots on plastic bags, while storks may incorporate old clothes and other rubbish into their massive nests.

Hooded crow

STRING
Small lengths are found in many nests.

METAL FOIL
Often collected by crows and magpies.

PLASTIC BALER TWINE
A favourite with birds nesting on farmland.

PAPER AND TISSUE
Found in the nests of many city birds.

Nest ingredients

Packed with a huge variety of ingredients, the pied wagtail's nest shown here is like a guide to a complete habitat. Its owner has scoured fields, hedgerows, old walls and fences for plant and animal materials, making hundreds or perhaps thousands of trips to bring all that it has collected back to the growing nest.

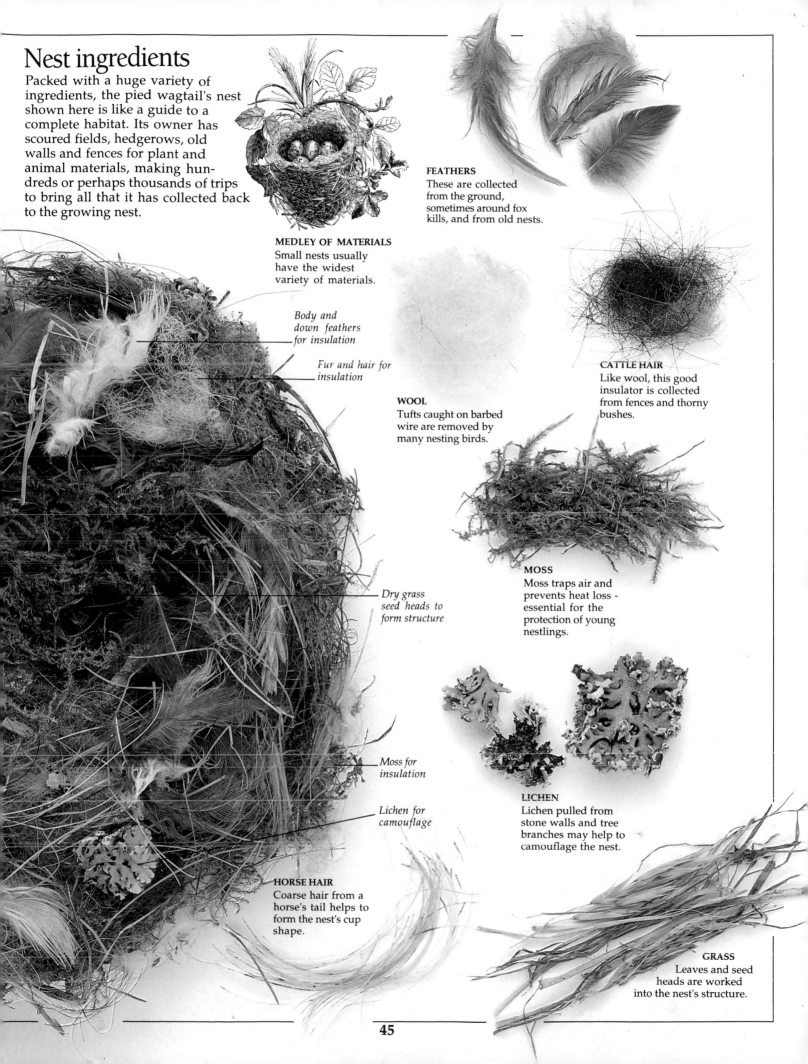

FEATHERS
These are collected from the ground, sometimes around fox kills, and from old nests.

MEDLEY OF MATERIALS
Small nests usually have the widest variety of materials.

Body and down feathers for insulation

Fur and hair for insulation

WOOL
Tufts caught on barbed wire are removed by many nesting birds.

CATTLE HAIR
Like wool, this good insulator is collected from fences and thorny bushes.

Dry grass seed heads to form structure

MOSS
Moss traps air and prevents heat loss - essential for the protection of young nestlings.

Moss for insulation

Lichen for camouflage

LICHEN
Lichen pulled from stone walls and tree branches may help to camouflage the nest.

HORSE HAIR
Coarse hair from a horse's tail helps to form the nest's cup shape.

GRASS
Leaves and seed heads are worked into the nest's structure.

Cup nests

Bird nests are immensely variable structures. They can be tiny shelves of saliva that are glued to the walls of caves, long tunnels that run many metres into the ground, or, in the case of some eagles, massive piles of branches that weigh more than a family-sized car. But the most familiar nests are undoubtedly the cup nests, which are built by birds of woodland, hedgerows and farmland. Despite their similarity in overall shape, the fine details of these nests identify their makers as surely as a fingerprint.

Rooks nesting on a weathervane

Chaffinch at nest

Moss and lichen cup forms the main structure of the nest

Feathers from other birds provide insulation

Hair and feather lining insulates the eggs and developing nestlings

Dried moss

Redstart

SPIDER'S WEB FOUNDATIONS
To make its nest, a chaffinch first loops strands of spiders' webs around a group of forked branches. These are the anchors for the nest, and having made sure that they are secure, the bird builds up the cup with moss, lichen and grass, finally lining it with feathers and hair. Collecting these nesting materials is a laborious task. If for any reason the chaffinch decides that its nest site is unsafe, it will transfer materials from the old nest to a new site to avoid too much extra work.

Song thrush feeding young

Mud lining

Outer cup

SECONDHAND FEATHERED LINING
Feathers are an important part of many birds' nests. Songbirds like the redstart, whose nest is shown here, collect feathers shed by other birds, while waterfowl and waders use their own feathers. Some small birds, such as sparrows, improve on the natural supply by pulling feathers from the backs of larger birds.

MASTERPIECE IN MUD
Many cup-nest builders use mud in constructing their nests, but in most cases it is applied as a layer just beneath a final lining of feathers, hair or grass. The song thrush is unusual in using mud as the lining itself. The bird makes a strong outer cup of twigs and grass, and then it smears the semi-liquid lining around the inside. Although mud makes up most of the mixture, it also contains saliva and animal droppings. Once the lining has been applied, it becomes hard. Even after the birds have left the nest it can withstand rain for many months.

Nests on buildings

Although it has taken birds millions of years to develop their nest-building skills, they are surprisingly quick to make use of any new sites that become available. Stone and brick houses are a relatively recent feature on the Earth. However, in the few thousand years that they have been in existence, some birds, particularly house martins, swifts, swallows and storks have taken up residence on them in large numbers. Walls and window-ledges make an ideal home for cliff-nesting birds; rooftops and chimneys are used by birds that originally nested in tree-tops; while kettles, shelves and tool-sheds are used by hedgerow species.

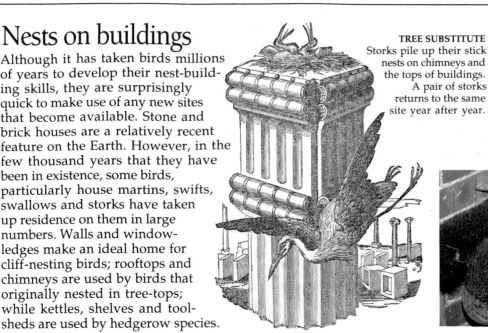

TREE SUBSTITUTE
Storks pile up their stick nests on chimneys and the tops of buildings. A pair of storks returns to the same site year after year.

ARTIFICIAL CLIFFS
Swallows and martins glue their mud nests onto ledges and vertical walls.

HEDGEROW HEIGHT
Hedge birds pick sites by height - this broom is right for a blackbird.

Nightingale with young

READY FOR RECYCLING
While some cup nests are carefully compacted, shaped and lined, others are less skilfully built. This nightingale's nest is made of reeds and grass. Loose nests like this may be dismantled by other birds for "recycling" after their owners have left them.

Lining made entirely of hair collected from ferns and bark against which animals have rubbed

Reeds

Loosely made structure of leaves, grass and reeds

Outer cup made of grass, leaves and stems matted together

A HAIR-FILLED NEST
Reed buntings build their small cup-shaped nests on or near the ground. The building bird (in this case, always the female) starts by making a frame of thick grass. Once this is finished, she adds the lining - a deep layer of fur or hair. This she plucks either from the thorns of hedgerow shrubs or from the barbs of barbed wire.

Grass lining on inside of cup

Female reed bunting at nest

Unusual nests

THE ANCESTORS of modern birds probably made nests that were simply depressions in the ground. Although some birds still do nest like this, others have elevated nest-building into a supreme craft, weaving nests of astounding complexity. But amazingly, none of these bird architects has any real understanding of what they are doing. Nest building is entirely instinctive; although a bird gets better with practice, it needs no training, and is incapable of departing from its blueprint.

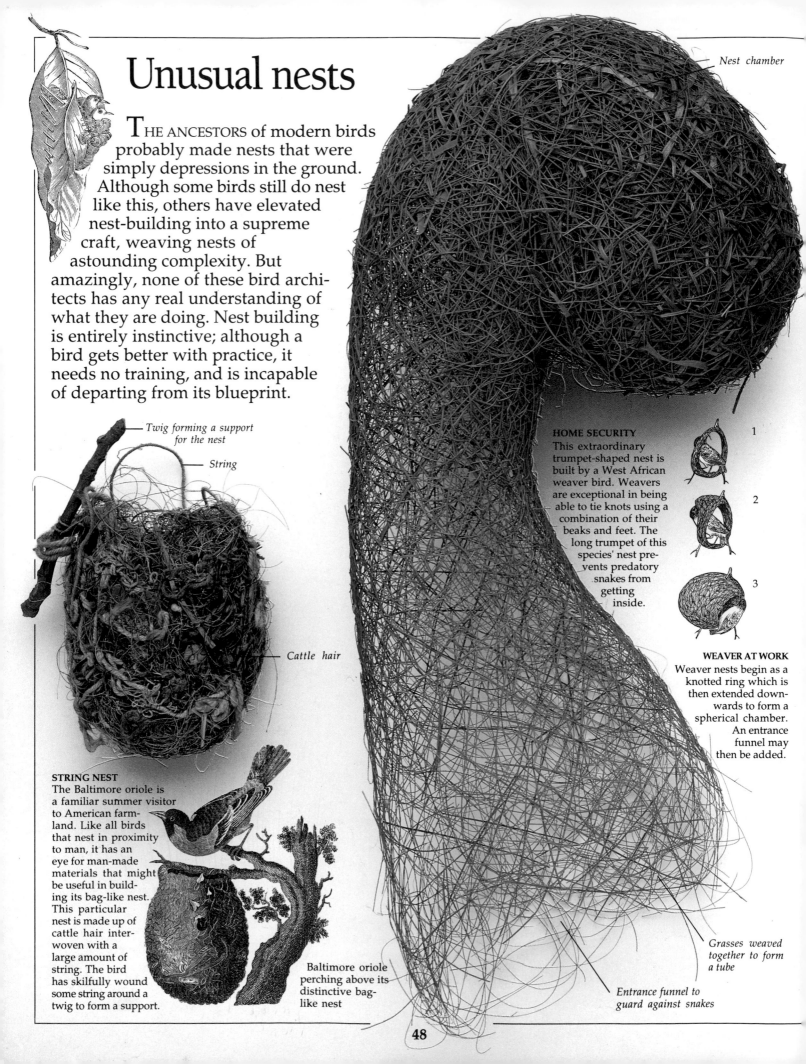

Twig forming a support for the nest

String

Cattle hair

Nest chamber

HOME SECURITY
This extraordinary trumpet-shaped nest is built by a West African weaver bird. Weavers are exceptional in being able to tie knots using a combination of their beaks and feet. The long trumpet of this species' nest prevents predatory snakes from getting inside.

1

2

3

WEAVER AT WORK
Weaver nests begin as a knotted ring which is then extended downwards to form a spherical chamber. An entrance funnel may then be added.

STRING NEST
The Baltimore oriole is a familiar summer visitor to American farmland. Like all birds that nest in proximity to man, it has an eye for man-made materials that might be useful in building its bag-like nest. This particular nest is made up of cattle hair interwoven with a large amount of string. The bird has skilfully wound some string around a twig to form a support.

Baltimore oriole perching above its distinctive bag-like nest

Grasses weaved together to form a tube

Entrance funnel to guard against snakes

SPLIT DUTIES

The male village weaver does nearly all the outside work in fashioning this elaborate bell-shaped nest. When the structure is complete, he flutters around the nest to entice a mate to inspect it. Once a female has approved his work and moved in, she completes the interior lining. By the time she is sitting on her clutch of eggs, the male will have started on a new nest. However, it is unlikely that he will move far away: like most weavers, the village weaver is a highly social bird - hundreds of individuals may build their nests in the same tree.

Thorn tree twig

Nest chamber

Entrance

Grass strands

Reed warbler with nestlings

Nest made of reed flowers, grasses and feathers

Reeds

A REEDBED BASKET

The reed warbler's nest is slung between dried stems deep in a reedbed. Building the cup-shaped nest calls for some acrobatic skill, particularly as the different stems to which the nest is attached often blow about in the wind. The nest is anchored with "handles" rather like those on a basket, and both male and female birds build on these foundations by adding reed flowers, grass and feathers.

MULTI-STOREY NEST

In reality, weavers' nests do not share the same entrance as suggested by this fanciful engraving.

Feathers

Interlocking mixture of moss, hair and spiders' webs

Entrance hole

Nest of penduline tit

CRAMPED QUARTERS

Although only about 18 cm (7 in) from top to bottom, the long-tailed tit's nest is one of the most elaborate outside the tropics. It is made up of spiders' webs, moss and hair, and is lined with hundreds of tiny feathers. However, it is so cramped that the female can fit inside only by curling her tail against the nest.

SHARED HOUSING

Colonial nests, although never quite this elegant, are built by a variety of birds.

Eggs of waterbirds and waders

THE KIND OF EGGS that birds lay depends on how they live. True seabirds (ones that only come ashore to breed) usually lay a single egg on rocky ledges away from predators. Wading birds lay more eggs, but, on the coasts and estuaries there is little cover for their nests, so their eggs are camouflaged.

Gulls

FOSTERED EGGS
A moorhen may "sneak" the first of its clutch of eggs into another bird's nest for the unsuspecting neighbour to look after. After this, it settles down to raise up to a dozen of its own eggs itself.

WARNING
All the eggs shown here come from established museum collections. Collecting or handling wild birds' eggs is now illegal.

Shoveler duck

A TERN'S EGGS
Little terns lay two or three eggs at a time in a depression in the ground, usually in shingle. The eggs' delicate patterning makes them almost indistinguishable from the surrounding pebbles.

Undersize egg

Normal egg

EGGS UNDER GUARD
Common tern eggs are fearlessly defended by their parents. During incubation, the birds attack any intruder - even humans - by diving directly at them.

VARIATIONS IN SIZE
Just as a litter of mammals may contain an undersize specimen, so occasionally may a clutch of eggs. These two eggs are both from a shoveler duck. Like most ducks, it produces a large number of eggs - between eight and 12 in a nest.

GULL EGGS
Many gulls lay their eggs on the ground, where camouflage is important. This egg is from one of the largest gulls, the great black-backed gull. Its speckled colour hides it from predators, which can include other gulls, during the four weeks it takes to hatch.

THE EGG THAT ROLLS BACK
The guillemot produces one of the most strikingly shaped and variably coloured eggs of all birds. Guillemots do not build nests. Instead, each female lays its single egg directly on to a bare cliff ledge. The egg's pointed shape helps to prevent her accidentally knocking it off its precarious niche. Should it begin to roll, it will travel back in a circle rather than on in a straight line. The different colours are more difficult to explain. They may help parents to recognize their own egg among the thousands in a guillemot colony.

Guillemot

Cream and brown form

White form

Streaked grey form

Egg from
speckled
clutch

Egg from
dark clutch

Egg from
light clutch

CAMOUFLAGE AND CONFUSION

The little ringed plover lays its eggs on gravel and shingle near water, where the eggs are protected by their camouflage colouring. If an intruder approaches the nest, the parent birds often fly directly at it, towards the source of danger, veering away at the last minute in an attempt to distract attention from the eggs. When the eggs have hatched, this distraction display becomes even more elaborate, with the parents scuttling away from the nestlings to confuse predators.

SLOW DEVELOPER

The fulmar's single egg needs an arduous seven-and-a-half weeks of incubation before it will hatch. The egg is laid on a cliff ledge, and its colour shows that there is little need for camouflage so far beyond the reach of land predators.

COLOURS IN A CLUTCH

Each of these three eggs comes from a small wading bird. Many camouflaged eggs vary widely in both pattern and colour between clutches. However, within a single clutch, the eggs are much more closely matched.

Snipe

THE DOUBLE-POINTED EGG

The great crested grebe lays its symmetrically shaped eggs on a mound of water-logged veg-etation. Most grebes have unusually pointed eggs - why is not known.

HEAVYWEIGHT WADER

Pointed at one end and blunt at the other, the curlew's egg is easy to identify. Like most waders, the curlew lays its clutch in a "scrape" on the ground.

Curlew

CONCEALED IN THE TREE-TOPS

The grey heron builds its nest high in the trees, so its blue eggs are rarely seen intact. When fresh, this specimen was bright blue, but the colour has faded over the years.

AT THE WATER'S EDGE

Divers are fish-eating birds of fresh water. They are clumsy on land, and so lay their dark brown eggs right by the water's edge to reduce the risk of damage.

RECORD INCUBATION

The albatross lays the largest and heaviest egg of any seabird, with some specimens weighing over 500 g (1.1 lb). Albatross eggs also have the longest incubation period of any bird: parents sit on a single egg for two-and-a-half months.

Albatross

Eggs of land birds

SMALL LAND BIRDS, like the seed- and insect-eaters, lay small eggs. However, many produce large clutches - sometimes well over a dozen - and others get through their breeding cycle very quickly and cram a number of clutches into a single season. Large birds, on the other hand, lay far fewer eggs. For birds such as eagles and vultures, one small clutch a year is all they produce.

Some of the specimens shown here have lost the intensity of their original colour due to age

HIDDEN IN THE UNDERGROWTH
The nightingale makes its nest in low tangled bushes. Its brown eggs are well hidden in the shadows cast by leaves and branches.

Coal tit egg

Blue tit egg

HEAVYWEIGHT CLUTCH
Tits, including the coal tit, blue tit and American chickadee, lay up to 15 eggs, each clutch weighing up to a third more than the bird.

Tawny owl egg

DOWN ON THE GROUND
Buntings are sparrow-like birds that lay their eggs on or near the ground. This is the egg of a corn bunting, a species unusual in that up to seven females may share the same mate.

Little owl egg

Wood warbler egg   Marsh warbler egg

SUMMER VISITORS
Most of the world's 400 species of warbler migrate to breed. Their arrival coincides with the annual insect population explosion, which provides food for the average family of six nestlings.

Chaffinch egg   Hawfinch egg

SLOW BEGINNERS
Finches lay betweeen four and six eggs in trees and bushes. Some finches do not lay eggs until early summer when seeds, their staple food, become available.

HIGHLY VISIBLE EGGS
Owl eggs are white, almost spherical, and have a glossy surface. The round shape is typical of many eggs laid in holes. The colour of owl eggs may be to enable the parent bird to see them, or alternatively, it may have evolved because there is no need for camouflage.

Long-eared owl

ADDED COLOUR
Surface colours like the brown and grey streaks on this Baltimore oriole's egg are formed just a few hours before the egg is laid.

Baltimore oriole

LESS TO LAY
The woodpigeon, a typical medium-sized bird, lays two eggs. Together, they weigh less than a tenth of the parent - a tiny pro- portion compared to the eggs of smaller birds.

THE CHIMNEY NESTER
The jackdaw, a member of the crow family, lays its eggs in holes, either in trees, rocky outcrops or buildings. Chimneys are one of its favourite nesting sites - sometimes with disastrous results.

Normal egg   Outsize egg

ABNORMAL EGGS
During the process of egg production, things sometimes go wrong. A single egg may have two yolks, or it may be of a different size to a normal egg. The eggs shown here are crow's eggs.

Carrion crow

MOORLAND CAMOUFLAGE
One look at a grouse's camouflaged egg shows that it is a ground-nester. Heavy blotches of colour help to conceal clutches of up to ten eggs during the month-long incubation among heather and bracken.

Cuckoo egg

Robin egg

THE CUCKOO'S DECEPTION
Cuckoos lay their eggs in the nests of other birds. The host birds are always much smaller than the cuckoo, and during the course of time, the cuckoo has evolved eggs that are tiny for a bird of its size. Here, a cuckoo has laid an egg among a robin's clutch.

Cuckoo

Dunnock egg

Cuckoo egg

A POOR MATCH
The European cuckoo has too many hosts to match all their eggs.

AMERICAN ROBIN
This bird is a member of the thrush family, unlike the European robin.

NON-STOP PRODUCTION
The blackbird's clutch of four eggs is typical of members of the thrush family. They all have the ability to raise more than one family in a year. If conditions are exceptionally good, a female blackbird can lay up to five clutches in a season. However, winter takes its toll of many of the offspring, and few survive into the following year.

DAYTIME DISGUISE
The nocturnal nightjar does not make a nest, and instead lays its pair of eggs on rough ground. The eggs' camouflage is almost as good as the parent bird's (p. 30).

HOLE-NESTER
Many woodpeckers chisel out nest holes in trees. Their eggs are very similar to those of hole-nesting owls - white and glossy.

RAISED AMONG THE ROOFTOPS
The kestrel lays a clutch of four to six eggs. It occasionally nests on city buildings, where its eggs perch precariously on gutters and window ledges.

VULNERABLE HAWKS
The sparrowhawk is currently recovering from damage caused by DDT. Although bright blue when laid, sparrowhawk eggs gradually fade.

FISH-EATING FALCON
The osprey - one of the most widely distrib-uted birds in the world - has eggs of exception-ally variable colour. They take about five weeks to be incubated.

OLD WORLD VULTURE
The Egyptian vulture lays its eggs high up on cliffs and in cave mouths. As an adult, it feeds on the eggs of other large birds, smashing them open with a stone.

ONE OF A PAIR
Eagles lay eggs in clutches of two. Unlike small birds, which lay an egg a day, eagles leave an interval of several days between laying the first and second egg.

SLOW DEVELOPERS
Buzzards lay between two and four eggs in a clutch. Incubation takes over five weeks and the nestlings stay in the nest for a further six weeks. As a result, parents can raise only one clutch a year.

Extraordinary eggs

THE LARGEST living bird, the ostrich, lays an egg which is 4,500 times heavier than that of the smallest, a hummingbird. But going back in time, one of the heaviest birds that ever existed - the elephant bird - laid eggs that could each have swallowed up seven ostrich eggs with room to spare. The extraordinary diversity in sizes of bird species is demonstrated particularly vividly by their eggs.

THE ROC
This creature from the *Arabian Nights* may have actually existed, not as a denizen of the air, but as the huge and flightless elephant bird of Madagascar.

HUMMINGBIRD EGG
Each egg weighs about one-fifth of the adult's weight.

OSTRICH EGG
Each egg weighs up to 1.5 kg (3.3 lb) - about one-hundredth of the adult weight.

Hummingbirds

LIGHTER THAN FEATHERS
Hummingbirds lay the smallest eggs of any bird. The very tiniest of them measures about 1 cm (0.4 in) from end to end and weighs about 0.35 g (0.01 oz). Hummingbird eggs have a pronounced cylindrical shape, and only two are laid in the tiny cup-shaped nest. It takes about three weeks for the nestlings to fledge and leave the nest to fend for themselves.

Shell almost 2 mm thick

CLUBBING TOGETHER
The ostrich lays the largest egg of any bird alive today. Although a single hen lays a clutch of about ten, more than one bird may lay in the same place, helping to create an unmanageable pile of perhaps as many as 50 eggs.

Ostrich

EMU EGG
The egg weighs just over one-hundredth of the adult's weight.

KIWI EGG
The egg is nearly one quarter of the adult's weight.

AN EGG THAT CHANGES COLOUR
When they are laid, the eggs of the Australian emu are a dull green colour, but within a few days they turn black and glossy. Like the ostrich, the emu is a prodigal parent. A nesting bird lays up to ten eggs weighing 700 g (1.5 lb) each.

Emu

THE KIWI'S OUTSIZE EGG
The chicken-sized kiwi lays the largest egg in proportion to her body of any bird. Each egg weighs about 450 g (1 lb) and normally the 1.7 kg (3.75 lb) female kiwi lays just one. Her labours are far from over once the egg has been laid: incubation lasts nearly two-and-a-half months.

Kiwi

ELEPHANT BIRD EGG
The egg weighed about three per cent of the adult's body weight.

THE LARGEST EGG
The bird that laid this monster egg - *Aepyornis titan* - or the "elephant bird", weighed nearly half a tonne, and its huge eggs tipped the scales at 12 kg (26 lb) each, making them the largest ever laid. Elephant birds lived in Madagascar, and although they died out about 700 years ago, whole eggs and shattered shells have been uncovered in the island's swamps. Elephant bird eggs easily outclass those of the dinosaurs - the volume of the bird's egg being over twice that of any dinosaur egg.

Hatching

FOR SOMETHING SO LIGHT, the shell of an egg is extremely strong, and a hatching bird must spend hours or even days of hard labour in breaching this barrier to the outside world. Some birds hatch in a poorly developed state. As nestlings, they are helpless and depend completely on their parents for food. However, "precocial" birds, such as the pheasant shown here, are well developed on hatching and can soon fend for themselves.

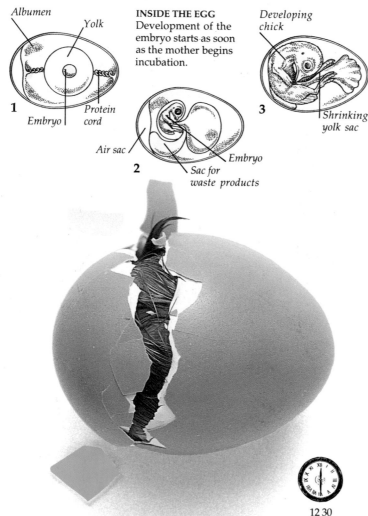

INSIDE THE EGG
Development of the embryo starts as soon as the mother begins incubation.

Albumen
Yolk
1
Embryo
Protein cord

Air sac
2
Sac for waste products
Embryo

Developing chick
3
Shrinking yolk sac

12 00

1 PREPARING FOR HATCHING
The prelude to hatching for a pheasant chick, like those of other birds, begins invisibly. The chick, still completely enclosed in the shell, turns around so that its beak is pointing towards the egg's blunt end. Then, with a sudden movement of its head, it pecks at the air sac. This is a crucial part of the chick's development because, by breaking into the sac, the chick is able to breathe air for the first time. Once its lungs are functioning, the chick may call to its mother from inside the egg. These calls probably help to prepare her for the onset of hatching.

12 30

4 COMPLETING THE CIRCLE
By hammering away at the shell, the chick has now almost detached the blunt end from the rest of the egg. Large pieces of shell fall away from the egg as the chick struggles to finish its labours. An entire clutch of pheasant eggs hatches within a few hours, so by the time the chick has reached this stage, its brothers and sisters will be well into the hatching process.

12 32

5 GETTING A GRIP
Having cut a complete circle through the shell, the chick begins to emerge from the egg. From now on, things happen very quickly. The chick first hooks its toes over the lip of the shell (the toes are just visible here), and then having got a good grip, it starts to push with its feet and shoulders. With a few heaves, the egg's blunt end is lifted away.

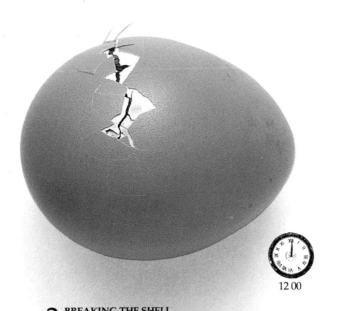

12 00

12 15

2 BREAKING THE SHELL

Hatching begins in earnest when, after several attempts, the chick finally breaks through the shell. It does this with the help of two special adaptations. The first is the "egg tooth", a small projection on its beak which breaks the shell and which falls off soon after hatching. The second is a powerful muscle behind the head which powers the egg tooth's blows. Between pecking sessions, the chick stops for long rests.

3 CUTTING A CIRCLE

Having broken open the shell, the chick sets about extending the initial crack sideways. After each bout of pecking, it stops and turns itself slightly by pushing with its feet. The chick's repeated pecking and turning produces a crack that runs neatly around the base of the egg's blunt end, and which will eventually allow the blunt end to be pushed away.

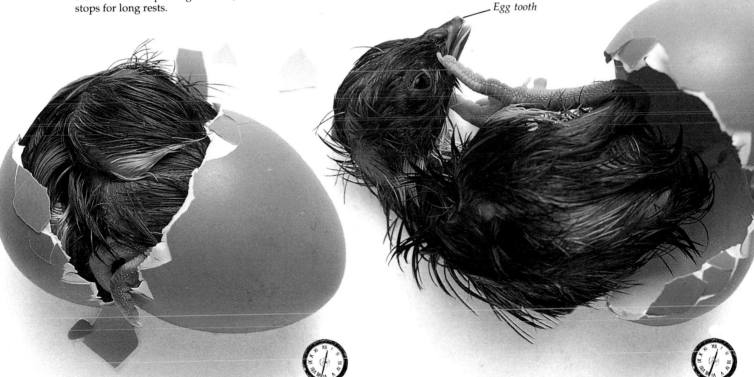

Egg tooth

12 32

12 33

6 BREAKING OUT

With its feet clearly visible, the chick gives another push and the blunt end of the egg comes away, sitting like a hat on the chick's head. This method of hatching, with the head emerging first, is shared by nearly all birds. The only exceptions are a few waders and other ground-living birds which either smash open their eggs in random pieces or kick their way out feet-first.

7 INTO THE OUTSIDE WORLD

With a final push, the chick tumbles out of the shell that has protected it during the three-and-a-half weeks of incubation. Within the next two hours, its feathers will dry and fluff up to provide an insulating jacket that will keep it warm. Once that has happened, the race is on to feed and grow. Pheasant chicks leave their nest almost immediately, and, amazing though it may seem, they are able to fly in only two weeks.

Growing up

GROUND-NESTING BIRDS hatch in a well-developed state (p. 56). However, the newly hatched young of many-tree- and hole-nesting birds are little more than bag-like feeding machines. They have well-developed digestive systems, but everything else about them - including even their eyes - is unifinished. This does not last for long. Fuelled by a staggering supply of food, nestlings like the blue tit's grow at a prodigious rate. The young of many species increase their weight by ten times in as many days, and their development is so rapid that they quickly catch up with birds that hatch fully fledged.

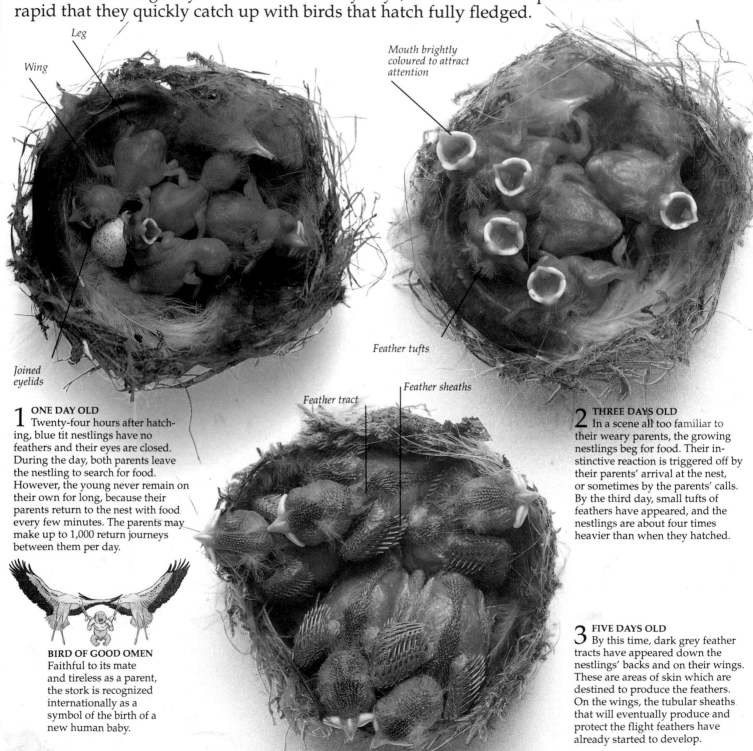

Wing

Leg

Joined eyelids

Mouth brightly coloured to attract attention

Feather tufts

Feather tract

Feather sheaths

1 ONE DAY OLD
Twenty-four hours after hatching, blue tit nestlings have no feathers and their eyes are closed. During the day, both parents leave the nestling to search for food. However, the young never remain on their own for long, because their parents return to the nest with food every few minutes. The parents may make up to 1,000 return journeys between them per day.

BIRD OF GOOD OMEN
Faithful to its mate and tireless as a parent, the stork is recognized internationally as a symbol of the birth of a new human baby.

2 THREE DAYS OLD
In a scene all too familiar to their weary parents, the growing nestlings beg for food. Their instinctive reaction is triggered off by their parents' arrival at the nest, or sometimes by the parents' calls. By the third day, small tufts of feathers have appeared, and the nestlings are about four times heavier than when they hatched.

3 FIVE DAYS OLD
By this time, dark grey feather tracts have appeared down the nestlings' backs and on their wings. These are areas of skin which are destined to produce the feathers. On the wings, the tubular sheaths that will eventually produce and protect the flight feathers have already started to develop.

Feather sheaths

Emerging feahter tips

ESCAPE FROM DANGER
Although most birds protect their nestlings by bluff or aggression when threatened, some parents can pick up their young and carry them away. Depending on the species, they may use either their beak, legs or talons.

EMERGENCY AIRLIFT
The woodcock is said to hold a chick between its legs while flying, although this has never been proved.

PINCER MOVEMENT
The secretive water rail carries its chicks in its long beak.

CARRIED IN TALONS
Some birds of prey, like the hawk, are thought to hold their nestlings in their talons.

4 NINE DAYS OLD
As the feather sheaths grow longer, the tips of the flight feathers themselves start to emerge. The areas of bare skin between the feather tracts have started to disappear, covered up by the growing feathers. The nest is starting to get crowded, although by blue tit standards, five nestlings is a relatively small family.

5 THIRTEEN DAYS OLD
At nearly two week, the nestlings are fully fledged and their eyes are open. Within another five days they will leave the nest, but the young birds will follow their parents for some time, begging for food as they gradually learn how to look after themselves. Full independence often comes when the paretns begin preparations for another clutch of eggs. Once the young birds find that their parents are ignoring their calls for food, they fend for themselves.

Attracting birds

IN WINTER, A ROOSTING BIRD like a robin can burn up a tenth of its body weight just in order to stay alive during the long hours of darkness. With each chill daybreak, the hungry bird must find food soon or die. So there is no better way to attract birds into your garden than by providing a regular supply of winter food. Seeds, nuts, fat, kitchen scraps and water will not only help the birds but will also enable you to watch them at close quarters. Having kept your garden birds alive during the winter, you can persuade many to stay for the summer by giving them somewhere to nest. As wild habitats disappear, nest boxes placed carefully beyond the reach of cats make valuable homes for a variety of birds.

Great and blue tits are attracted by nuts and fat at bird tables

CALL OF THE WILD
Birds have an innate distrust of humans, but St Francis of Assisi (here depicted in stained glass) is said to have had a special attraction for birds.

Sloping lid to throw off rainwater

Hole 29 mm (1.14 in) across keeps out large birds

Perching post

GABLED BOXES
A roof gives nestlings protection against rain, but it also reduces air circulation. Nest boxes should not be placed where they will be in direct sunlight.

SIMPLE HOLE-FRONTED BOXES
This straightforward design appeals to woodland birds such as tits and nuthatches. The small hole keeps out inquisitive sparrows.

Hinged lid

OPEN-FRONTED BOXES
Robins, flycatchers, wrens and wagtails prefer nest boxes that give them a good view when incubating. These birds usually nest in thick vegetation, so the box needs to be well concealed. This will also help to protect the residents from cats.

FANCY BOXES
What appeals to humans doesn't necessarily appeal to birds. Bird boxes with unnecessary ornaments may actually deter birds looking for a home. If you do choose a "house box" like this, first make sure that it is solidly constructed. Then check that it can be cleaned and that the roof really will keep rainwater out of the nesting chamber.

Removable lid for inspecting nest

Two halves of a log hollowed out and nailed together to make the nesting chamber

LOG BOXES
A hollowed-out log makes an excellent home for small woodland birds. This box does not have a perching post, but the bark around the entrance hole is rough enough to give a bird a good toe-hold when landing or taking off.

Feeding table may attract other birds, disturbing those nesting in the box

MEALWORMS
Insect-eating birds find these beetle grubs quite irresistible. Mealworms can be raised in containers filled with bran.

Fat and seed ball

SEED CAKES AND PUDDINGS
Of all the kinds of food that you can give garden birds, oils and fats are the richest in energy. All seeds have oils in them, but they can be pressed together with more oil or fat to make a real bird banquet. This way of feeding birds has another advantage. Because the food is in a solid lump, birds cannot fly away with it, giving you plenty of opportunity to watch them at their meal.

Great spotted woodpecker feeding on peanuts

Screw-fit lid for refilling

Commercial "bird pudding"

Seed cake

Peanuts

Perching post

Coconut, a winter food for acrobatic blue tits

Wire mesh keeping nuts in and large birds out

LOOSE SEED
Mixtures of loose seed are an excellent food, although birds such as tits may fly away with the larger seeds, to eat them out of sight.

Hunger sometimes forces birds to overcome shyness in winter

NUT DISPENSER
Natural, *unsalted* peanuts are popular with tits and greenfinches. A hanging dispenser helps to keep larger birds at bay.

BREAD
Although not an ideal food for birds, bread makes a useful stopgap. Brown bread makes a far better bird food than white.

Watching birds

IN EUROPE ALONE, including annual migrants, there are probably about 600 species of birds. An experienced birdwatcher may recognize any one of these given no more than a distant silhouette or just a few seconds of song. This skill can seem baffling, but it is simply the result of careful observation - looking at the shape and colour of birds, and also watching the way they live.

Getting close to wild birds requires skill and patience

WARNING
When watching birds, always avoid disturbing them. Be particularly careful when watching or photographing parent birds with their young.

KEEPING A NOTEBOOK
Field guides are essential for identifying birds, but keeping a notebook is the best way to train your eye to look for a bird's key features. Sketching plumage, flight patterns and noting behaviour will all help to build up your knowledge.

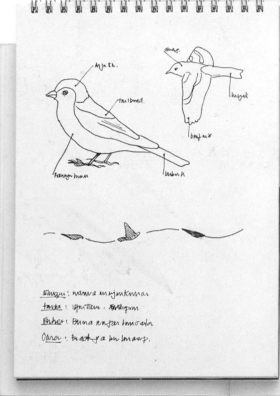

SKETCHING EQUIPMENT
You don't have to be an artist to draw birds. A collection of coloured pencils will enable you to sketch details instead of writing lengthy notes.

Objective lens

Ruler for measuring feathers

Eyepiece lens

BINOCULARS
Serious birdwatching is almost impossible without a good pair of binoculars, but good does not necessarily mean tremendously powerful. For birdwatching, binoculars should be light and have good magnification together with a fairly wide field of view. Heavy binoculars are cumbersome, and if they magnify more than ten times the field of view is narrow, and the image very wobbly - this can make locating moving birds very difficult. Binoculars are graded by the diameter of the objective lens and the magnification. One of the best combinations of size and magnification for birdwatching is the 8 x 30.

Magnifying glass

Plastic tweezers are less likely to damage fine bones than metal ones

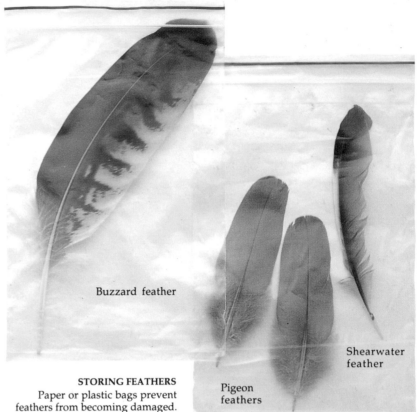

Buzzard feather

Pigeon feathers

Shearwater feather

STORING FEATHERS
Paper or plastic bags prevent feathers from becoming damaged.

EQUIPMENT FOR EXAMINING PELLETS
Many of the animal remains inside bird pellets (p. 42) are very delicate and are easily damaged when a pellet is pulled apart. By using a magnifying glass and a pair of tweezers, small bones and teeth can be separated from fur and feathers without breakage.

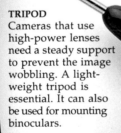

Camera mounting

USING A HIDE
Birds are quick to detect movement, but will ignore stationary objects, no matter how incongruous they seem to human eyes. Even on flat, open ground birds will accept a hide as a natural feature and approach it without any fear.

TRIPOD
Cameras that use high-power lenses need a steady support to prevent the image wobbling. A light-weight tripod is essential. It can also be used for mounting binoculars.

CHOOSING LENSES
With a standard 50 mm lens, birds often appear small and indistinct. A telephoto lens produces a much larger image.

200 mm tele-photo lens

CAMERAS FOR BIRD PHOTOGRAPHY
A 35 mm SLR camera is ideal for photographing birds because the image can be seen exactly through the viewfinder. Taking pictures of wild birds - especially in flight - *is* difficult. Practise approaching the subject, focussing rapidly and steadying the camera with garden birds before venturing further afield.

Index

Acknowledgments

Dorling Kindersley would like to thank:
Philip Amies; the staff of the Natural History Department, City of Bristol Museum; the staff of the British Museum (Natural History) at Tring; Martin Brown of the Wildfowl Trust, Slimbridge; and Rosemary Crawford for their advice and invaluable help in providing specimens.
Steve Parker and Anne-Marie Bulat for their work on the initial stages of the book.
Fred Ford and Mike Pilley of Radius Graphics, and Ray Owen and Nick Madren for artwork.
Tim Hammond for editorial assistance.

Publishers' note
No bird has been injured or in any way harmed during the preparation of this book.

Picture credits
t=top b= bottom m= middle l=left r=right

R. Austing/Frank Lane Picture Agency: 32br
A.P. Barnes/Planet Earth Pictures: 15m
Jen & Des Bartlett/ Survival Anglia: 54br
Leo Batten/Frank Lane Picture Agency: 39m
G.I. Bernard/NHPA: 21ml, mr
Tony & Liz Bomford/Ardea London: 14mr
Bridgeman Art Library: 13tr; 28tr; 52t; 61b
C. Carvalho/Frank Lane Picture Agency: 17t
Manfred Danegger/NHPA: 13m
Mary Evans Picture Library: 6bl, br; 9 tr, mr; 10t, mr, b; 20bl; 24t; 26t; 30mr; 32m; 36t, mr; 38t; 41t; 54tl, tr, bl; 56t; 58b
J. K. Fawcett/Frank Lane Picture Agency: 12mr
Jeff Foott/Survival Anglia: 31mr

T. & P. Gardner/Frank Lane Picture Agency: 21bl
Sonia Halliday: 60tr
Brian Hawkes/Robert Harding: 47t
John Hawkins/Eric & David Hosking: 13tl; 19tl; 35m
Peggy Heard/Frank Lane Picture Agency: 61m
David Hosking: 16t; 35tr; 37bl; 47m; 60m
Eric Hosking: 33b; 63
Eric & David Hosking: 12bl; 14m; 29t, ml; 37tl; 46m
Roger Hosking/Eric & David Hosking: 60tl
Hellio & Van Ingen/NHPA: 40b
R. Jones/Frank Lane Picture Agency: 17m
Frank W. Lane: 37mr
Gordon Langsbury/Bruce Coleman Ltd: 13b; 14b
Michael Leach/NHPA: 34m
Mansell Collection; 6t, 10ml; 34t; 54m
Pickhall Library: 15t
Press-Tige Pictures: 12mr
Derek A. Robinson/Frank Lane Picture Agency: 8m; 47b

H. Schrempp/Frank Lane Picture Agency: 32bl
Sinclair Stammers/Science Photo Library: 6m
Roger Tidman/Frank Lane Picture Agency: 37tr
B.S. Turner/ Frank Lane Picture Agency: 42t
R. Van Nostrand/Frank Lane Picture Agency: 37br
John Watkins/Frank Lane Picture Agency: 33ml
Philip Wayre/NHPA: 19br
Roger Wilmshurt/Bruce Coleman Ltd: 15b
Roger Wilmshurst/Frank Lane Picture Agency: 12br; 46t; 49t
W. Wisniewski/Frank Lane Picture Agency: 37ml
J. Zimmermann/Frank Lane Picture Agency: 31tr; 36b

Illustrations by: Mick Loates of Linden Artists, Coral Mula and Will Giles.

Picture reseach by: Millie Trowbridge.